The
Plateauing
Trap

THE PLATEAUING TRAP

How to Avoid It in Your Career . . . and Your Life

Judith M. Bardwick, Ph.D.

AMERICAN MANAGEMENT ASSOCIATION

This book is available at a special
discount when ordered in bulk quantities.
For information, contact Special Sales Department,
AMACOM, a division of American Management Association,
135 West 50th Street, New York, NY 10020.

Library of Congress Cataloging-in-Publication Data

Bardwick, Judith M., 1933-
    The plateauing trap.

Includes index.
    1. Career plateaus.   I. Title.
HF5384.5.B36   1986   650.1'4   86-47583
ISBN 0-8144-5871-8

Printing number

10 9 8 7 6 5 4 3 2 1

This book
is dedicated to my husband,
Allen E. Armstrong,
Captain, United States Coast Guard, Ret.

Introduction

You cannot look at someone's life and know whether that person is plateaued. In some ways, being plateaued—reaching a stage in work or in life where there is no more growth or movement—is a fact. But more than that, it's a feeling, a psychological state, not always visible to outsiders. People who are very busy and successful can *feel* plateaued, and others, who are not successful in the usual ways, can be satisfied with life. I know, from very personal experience.

No one looked less plateaued than me when I went to California in 1981 on a sabbatical. I was a professor in one of the leading psychology departments in the country. Over the previous 20 years I had never stopped researching and writing on the cutting edge of my field. But when I began the year of the sabbatical I knew that inside I was twitchy and discontent. I alternated periods of knowing what was wrong with periods of denying that anything was wrong. Mostly, I summed it up with, "I'm tired of working." I didn't feel despair and I wasn't powerfully depressed. I just wasn't really happy.

Before that year my career had taken me from half-time lecturer to full professor and associate dean of the College of Literature, Science and Art at the University of Michigan, one of the most prestigious schools in the country. Over the years I had made a name for myself in my specialty, but after working in it for so long, I began to feel that my most creative period was in the past. So, when I was offered the opportunity to become an associate dean, I readily agreed; I'd never done anything like that before.

The first year as an administrator was wonderful. I had to make a lot of decisions and I didn't know anything. Did I learn! The second year I was more effective because I knew a lot, but the problems were starting to sound familiar. The third year was awful—I had seen every problem before. Also, the budget crunch was terrible so we weren't creating anything. By then it was not only repetitive, it was kind of dreary.

During this period, when it was becoming clear that I was good at creating administrative programs but no good at running them, I chanced upon a new mega-problem that no one had heard very much about. The problem was plateauing. I was delighted to have a new, tough issue to work on. I knew, of course, that work was not life. Still, it seemed it was only in my work, where I had control, that I could create the beginnings that gave my life vitality.

By the time I arrived in California for the sabbatical I had spent two years researching and writing on the subject of plateauing. During the first year I had published some papers and given some workshops, but most people told me that I was exaggerating the problem, yelling, like Chicken Little, that the sky was falling down while they could see it firmly overhead. In the second year, there was much more recognition that the issue was important.

When I didn't have to fight so hard for acceptance of my work, I began to look at the rest of my life. I slowly realized that I was in the midst of exactly what I had been researching. While telling corporations and their managements about the problems of plateauing, I was standing on a plateau of my own.

La Jolla, California, is as different from Ann Arbor, Michigan, as one can imagine. It sits on the edge of the Pacific, in a climate that is almost perfect. Although I worked hard in California, I found that I had slipped into a lifestyle where there was time for friends, for athletics, for walking on the beach—for aspects of life that had nothing to do with work. That was a revelation, and it was delicious. Reluctant to give it up, the next year I accepted a position as a visiting professor of business in a university in San Diego, and took a leave of absence from Michigan. In the winter of that second year, Michigan said, "Come home!" What they actually said was, "Fish or cut bait."

Could I stay? In the year as a visiting professor, I had learned that there was no appropriate academic department for me in San Diego. I was a professor and there was no obvious way I could earn a living. If I remained in California, I would have no economic security, no status, no power, no nothing. On the other hand, I had used Ann Arbor up. There were no experiences I could have there that I had not already had.

I don't remember any decision as difficult as that one. Stay, or go back? The ratio was 49:51, and the 2 percent switched back and forth like a pendulum as my head wrestled with the alternatives. Prudence told me to return; my viscera told me not to. People besieged me with advice. Some thought I was crazy and irresponsible even to think about not returning; others were very enthusiastic.

In the six months I spent deciding, the requests for lectures and workshops on plateauing picked up. I decided I had already eaten filet and now I could eat peanut butter. So I resigned.

Michigan was shocked, but I was relieved. Then I felt happy. That gave me a surge of energy, so I worked better than before. Business prospered, and I decided to become a full-time corporate consultant. When I made the commitment to stay, I felt closer to my friends and they to me. At the age of 50 I had ended my lifelong career, started a new one, moved to a new part of the country, and set down roots.

I know that it was very scary to end so much and start so much. But the truth is that now I cannot recall what that fear was like. Actually, I don't think I have ever felt much regret about anything I've done; my regrets are for the things I didn't do. Staying in California involved a lot of risk, but for me there was more risk in going back to a life I knew much too well. If I had gone back, I would always regret not knowing how my new life might have turned out.

When we are plateaued, we are not so much actively unhappy as we are just not happy. We could continue to live as we are, because usually it's not awful. But it is also not joyous. If we are truly unhappy, change is easier than when we are just not happy. When the negative is powerful, the need to change is obvious. Most of us do not make changes in our lives until the pain in the present eclipses our fear of the future, just as it did for me.

If after reading this book, you think you are plateaued, you will feel a sense of relief, because you will understand what is happening to you. But you may also feel frightened, because you will have come to the realization that you need to change your life—and that is scary. There is always a lot of risk when you undertake a major change in your life. If the change is in work, you can be afraid that you will lose what you have gained and you will never win in the race again. If the change is a personal one involving the end of a relationship or the beginning of one, you can be afraid of losing love and the emotional security of knowing where you belong.

We can speak to the negative, of what the consequences might be if you don't change. Although you can remain secure in the life you know, it will lack zest. Then you could spend the rest of your life wondering what might have been. That seems a poor way to live.

We can also speak to the positive, of what the consequences could be if, when you are plateaued, you *do* change. Constructive change is usually evolutionary; it does not involve throwing out all your old commitments and denying your history. Constructive change means giving up patterns of attitudes and living that often served you well in the past but now, in the present, no longer do. It involves a process of growth: expanding your capabilities, changing your values, and broadening your involvements so that there are many more sources of good experiences.

Everyone plateaus in one form or another, and most people plateau more than once. Few have the opportunity or the desire to solve that problem in the extreme way that I did. The majority must find some workable compromise in the reality of their opportunities and responsibilities. That is why I have focused more on change within organizations than within individuals, because most people need to create something better in the workplace, where they spend most of their time.

I have written this book to give you and your company an awareness of plateauing so that you can recognize it, manage it, and discover the opportunity that it provides. This is for everyone facing the challenge of change, and the desire to move from the plateau to a more fulfilling experience of life.

Acknowledgments

I would like to take this opportunity to thank those people who have been of immense help to me. Some helped by encouraging me to work on the subject of plateauing, assuring me that it was an important issue long before the problem had become obvious. Some people helped by hiring me to address the issue in their organizations, long before the corporation was willing to admit it had a plateauing problem. Some helped by reading the manuscript, telling me what was okay and what was not. To all I give many thanks. In alphabetical order, they are:

Allen E. Armstrong, Captain, United States Coast Guard, Ret.

Robert F. Barry, PhD, Director of Artificial Intelligence, Westinghouse.

Harry Bernhard, formerly program manager of management development, IBM, now Harvard Business School IBM Fellow.

Timothy A. Boone, Ph.D., partner, Kielty, Goldsmith and Boone.

Walter Green, president and CEO, Harrison Conference Services.

Stephen Hardis, vice chairman, Eaton Corporation.

Winthrop Knowlten, chairman of Harper & Row and department chairman at the John F. Kennedy School of Government at Harvard.

Michael Marchese, IBM management development instructor.

Paul McCracken, PhD, Edmund Ezra Day University Professor of Business Administration at the University of Michigan.

Norman Schoenfeld, group vice president, Wickes Manufacturing.

Contents

1

What Is Plateauing and Why Is It So Important?

Plateauing is a natural phenomenon that occurs, in its different forms, in all the phases of our lives. Being plateaued does not, therefore, have to be experienced as a state of failure. Instead, it can be viewed as a period of challenge. Being plateaued can prod us into creating new goals that are significant and achievable. Being plateaued should be a phase, not a permanent state.

At one time or another, most of us will plateau in our work or in our lives. We can look upon the plateau as a chance to renew ourselves, to increase our self-knowledge and self-acceptance, to reaffirm our values or create new ones, and gain a more lasting kind of success.

I first became aware of plateauing in the late 1970s when I reconnected with friends I had met in the early part of that decade. They were middle managers in one of the largest and most prestigious corporations in the United States and I was a professor at the University of Michigan. When we first became acquainted they were so proud of their organization and so wrapped up in their work that I was very impressed. They were also so well paid and generally cared for by the corporation that I was jealous. I even thought about leaving the university and going to work for the same organization.

Then we lost contact for about six years. When we met again, it was totally different. Now they were bitter toward the corporation and talked about leaving it. Some were actually looking around for new ways to earn a living and, after a year or two, they moved on. I couldn't understand what they were so angry about. They were middle managers, not even executives; here I was, a professor and associate dean, being paid one-third of what they were, with few of the elegant benefits.

The tone of their anger had a particular quality that was intriguing. They felt betrayed. It was the same kind of emotion one sees in people who feel that their family has broken faith and betrayed their commitment. They couldn't tell me why they were so bitter; it took several months to piece together an explanation.

When I first met them, they believed that everyone was getting promoted every 18 to 24 months. Now, they said, *"If you get promoted at all, it takes eight years."* It seemed the chase for success had ended, and now they were forced to look at what they had paid to gain success. Without further promotions, the cost—in terms of how they had lived—seemed too great. The corporation-as-family had promised that if they gave most of their lives to it, winning would never end. Now they felt a bitter sense of betrayal. The corporation was still the largest commitment in their lives, and they still gave it more time and psychological energy than anything else. They felt that they had kept their part of the bargain, but the organization had broken its word.

> This is a good company and I have to be fair and say that it's been pretty good to me. But I earned that. I've worked damn hard. Right now it bothers me that even though my assignments get bigger, my grade doesn't. Without a promotion, I'm not really sure what they think of me. They keep saying I'm terrific. Now let them show me.

> For a long time I got promoted every couple of years, then it slowed down. Now it's been about six years since the last one. I guess I'd better face it—maybe there's one more, maybe there's no more. I wonder if my perception of myself is the same as the others. I think I have a lot more to offer.

My friends had become classic examples of people who are *plateaued*. They had reached a stage in their lives, specifically in their careers, where they were blocked and could not see any way to reach the next step.

Plateauing creates problems for people and thus for their organizations. Especially for those who have been successful, who have been winners, being plateaued can destroy motivation, allegiance, commitment, and productivity.

A Quick Look at Plateauing

Plateauing is a concept that says *when a major aspect of life has stabilized, as it ultimately must, we may feel significantly dissatisfied.* The essential source of the dissatisfaction is that the present is not engrossing and the future is not clear. There is not yet an answer to the question "What will I do next?" People who are plateauing are at a level—they are neither rising nor falling.

Most individuals and organizations don't recognize that kind of plateauing as a problem, at least not for them. It hasn't commanded much attention until now, and the concepts and the facts are not widely known, so it's hard for people to begin to talk about it. Instead of being a clear problem, it tends to manifest itself as a vague but pervasive feeling that things are not okay. In itself, this vagueness makes it harder for people to identify the problem, much less deal with it. But as soon as the words, ideas, and facts are on the table, there is a near-universal response of *aha!* People say, "Yes, *that's* what's been going on. I didn't want to talk about it before but since you brought the subject up, I can begin to think about dealing with it." Transforming a vague anxiety into a specific problem is always the first step to solving the problem.

The vagueness also stems from peoples' reaction to the word itself; they say that it makes them uncomfortable. But plateauing is a neutral word; it describes a status. There is nothing intrinsically bad about that. Plateauing is one phase of the process of change that characterizes everyone's life. In one form or another, everyone plateaus, and over the course of a lifetime, almost everyone plateaus more than once. When you recognize that you are plateaued, that awareness can make being plateaued the platform upon which to build the next phase of life.

Plateauing is thus an essentially simple phenomenon, but it becomes complicated when organizations and individuals find their most central values challenged by its occurrence. When people are plateaued, their growth ambitions, which formed the central themes of their being, are no longer assets because they cannot be achieved. Then the frustrations spill out over everything that is most important—peoples' identity, their sense of self-esteem, their relationships, their performance, and their future . . . in short, everything that counts.

What's a Plateaued Person?

In the course of every workshop I conduct, I ask the participants to call out the words and phrases that come to mind when they think of plateaued people. I never give them the words, and they never fail to provide them. The words and phrases are vivid and piercingly judgmental; the image they portray is inescapable. Without coaching, the audience says that someone who is plateaued is:

in the closet	walking	when you get
peaked	wounded	close enough,
coasting	on the shelf	you hear an
out of runway	out of the run-	echo
a shelf sitter	ning	a goofoff
obsolescent	incompetent	playing defense
on an in-plant	a coat rack	POPO (pissed on
vacation	lack-a-wanna	and passed
a *Wall Street*	dead wood	over)
Journal retiree	slug	burned out
a spare wheel	moss-back	a spare wheel
old what's-his-	over the hill	retired in place
name	pumping gas	rocks
an empty suit	out to lunch	cadavers

As people call the words out there's usually a lot of laughing. Many of the terms are indeed funny, but this humor is hostile. Then slowly the laughter stops and the room gets quiet. Secret fears about being plateaued have been triggered, and people sit rigidly, thinking, "My god, they're talking about me."

Where the Disappointment Comes From

The psychological basis for the profound disappointment that may accompany plateauing lies in our optimistic, expansionistic view. Most of us define success in terms of getting more: more power, more money, more responsibility, more prestige. For many of us, that kind of upward mobility has, in fact, been real. Our expectations of ever-increasing success have been realized, so past success creates the desire for more.

For a long time, history was on the side of the ambitious. From 1950 to 1975, we experienced an extraordinary period of economic expansion. American businesses dominated world markets, and it seemed that there were no limits to what we could achieve. During this period, organizations expanded hugely; governments, universities, hospitals, and other institutions doubled in size, and corporations increased by 56 percent. The major problem for organizations was finding enough qualified people to fill the managerial slots. Most of the labor force then was born around the Depression, when the birthrate was the lowest in our history. And, relative to now, few people went to college.

As a result, those who performed well were promoted unusually swiftly. People's primary goal soon became gaining promotion. If people worked in a large and complex organization, the possibilities for promotion seemed limitless when they looked up the hierarchical ladder. Increasingly, all rewards were tied to promotion, promotions were certainly possible, and *promotion became the only meaningful reward.*

Twenty-five years is a generation, long enough for people to think that's the way things always were. Today's expectations about careers are based on that extraordinary period in recent history. Unfortunately, we cannot meet those expectations. Today we're in another unique period—the exact opposite of the previous one.

The Current Situation, and the Future

Now, and for some time into the future, far fewer people will experience the "success" of promotion. The economic prosperity of the postwar period has proved unsustainable; our economy is experiencing severe withdrawal pains. What this means for today's employees is devastatingly simple: opportunities for promotion will become relatively scarce, until at least the end of this century.

The fundamental factors that determine overall rates of promotion are impersonal; they have nothing to do with personal competence and they cannot be changed by any individual. But people don't think about that; they still keep score in terms of how they as individuals fare in the competition. From 1950 to 1975, ambition and performance paid off in promotion. Since not everyone was promoted at the same rate, it was easy to focus on the ability of the individual. Anyone who was smarter, gutsier, luckier, and harder-working kept on receiving promotions. The individual was in the foreground. Relatively few noted that in the background increasing numbers of opportunities were continuously being created. The impersonal factors worked in people's favor then. But not now.

Today the individual is still in the perceptual foreground. We still pay attention to how well someone is doing relative to others. Few people pay much attention to the demographic and economic forces in the background that are causing extraordinary competition among a huge number of unusually well-qualified candidates.

Unlike that earlier golden time, today's organizations are not expanding rapidly. And we have the largest population of educated and qualified people competing for positions in our history. The number of positions is not expanding nearly as rapidly as the number of qualified candidates. The effects of the slower rate of organizational expansion and of the increased competition created by the educated baby-boomers is already being felt in companies of all kinds. Competition is crueler and plateauing occurs earlier. Although that is harsh, it is also, in a sense, a good thing. Until the problem became so bad that it was undeniable, few organizations did anything about it.

Organizations operate with the same ambitions as individuals do. Managers of most organizations are obsessed with growth. They feel compelled to achieve uninterrupted expansion in sales, profits, markets, and size. "Their world revolves around comparisons with the previous year and the last quarter, and even around variances on a monthly basis. Like new parents who weigh the baby several times daily and count each ounce gained as a triumph, they think bigger is better . . . growth is a cultural value: a company that is not expanding is said to be falling behind. A stigma is associated with the failure to grow."[34]

Plateauing creates the most problems in mature organizations, because they are no longer expanding rapidly and are, therefore, not creating the new positions that produce mobility. To make things worse, management opportunities have actually declined in the past two to three years. Faced with increased world competition in the terrible recession that began in 1982, many mature organizations have severely trimmed their ranks of middle management and seem inclined to stay lean. Yet many of these organizations have ignored the plateauing issue because it is tied to their "failure" to continue heady growth.

The current situation demands that we take another look at promotion and organizational structure. Up to now, people have designed their lives around work and articulated their ambitions in terms of promotion. Winning this race is everything; all else is secondary. In the relatively recent past, people started losing in this promotion game when they approached their personal limitations. Now, and into the future, people will stop "winning" long *before* they approach their limits.

Plateauing is the source of widespread tragedy in American business. That tragedy is wholly logical, and wholly unnecessary. More than anything, people with a history of success at work want to continue being promoted. But the essential fact is that virtually everyone who works in an organization will plateau. The only difference among people is how long they take to reach the level beyond which they will not rise. Because very few are psychologically prepared for the end of the climb, most people experience pain. If they don't understand what is happening to them, anxiety is added to their depression.

Relatively few managers, professionals, and executives know why promotion has become for them the only organizational response that means success. And only a few fully realize that between now and the year 2015, promotions must become scarcer and the rate of plateauing will increase; people will plateau much earlier in their careers than they have for almost three decades. If they knew the facts and understood what was happening to them, they could be psychologically prepared. Most need to redefine success but have neither the information nor the perspective that comes from knowing the facts. As a result, promotion continues to be the single most important criterion of success. Unprepared, most people don't understand why they are failing to reach higher levels. In many cases, this is compounded by their organization's failure to be honest about their long-term prospects.

As long as people don't change what is important to them—as long as promotion is the only outcome that counts—many will be frustrated. When people change what they value so they have goals that are both important and achievable, they can be satisfied.

Coming to Terms with Plateauing

We all know that it's terrific to achieve something, but that pleasure is usually short-lived. *Being there* is not nearly as satisfying as *getting there*. Each promotion results in more responsibilities and incremental recognition, and each promotion is the preparation for the next. It's the climbing that is heady.

Because people have come to regard promotion as the only reward for performance that really counts, only promotion signifies winning. Psyched up to want only one thing, people are in danger of feeling no longer successful when promotions end. In the extreme, people can feel like failures.

In January 1986, on the editorial page of *The Wall Street Journal*, Robert Goldman described his own experience:

> I am 42 years old. I work for a large corporation. But I'm no longer moving up.
>
> Going in, I knew there could be a price to pay. Too much structure can be confining. But for me, the organizational chart was like a children's playground—a place to climb, swing, and scramble all the way to the top.
>
> And that was where I was headed. After all, isn't that what it's all about?
>
> Year by year, level by level, I made my way up; and if I wasn't laughing all the way, only rarely did I doubt choosing the corporate life.
>
> Whatever the reason, I was immediately perceived to be a "star." And though my corporation was too conservative to have a "fast track," I did burn a few cinders as a steady progression of blue memos charted my upward progress.
>
> Over the years I gained titles, windows, salary and perks. Those incentives fueled a fire that was burning very bright indeed. I knew in my bones that I would someday reach the top. Some men might stumble. Others might even fall by the wayside. But not me; never me.
>
> Or so I believed, right up to the day, right up to the instant, when I learned the fire was out, the star was extinguished, the climb was over.
>
> A promotion that should have been mine was handed to someone else. When the blue memo came out,

I could hardly believe my eyes. How could the corporation make this mistake?

Betrayed, vulnerable, I began seeing corporate assassins in the shadows. Predators lurked outside my office; measuring, measuring.

Finally I took my fears to a friend on Mahogany Row.

"Everyone is happy with your work," I was reassured. "Just keep doing what you're doing."

Which was exactly what I did.

And when the next promotion came up, and again, the blue memo did not come for me, I finally understood.

Somewhere along the line, a test had been given, and I had failed. The corporation would keep me on. I would do my job, and in return, I could expect the average salary increases due the average employee. But there would be no more leap-frog advancements. No more seductive little perks. No more blue memos.

I was no longer climbing. I had plateaued out.

I can't say I have come to accept my situation, nor can I bring myself to believe I will never reach the top. Whether this is the spirit that makes America great, or total immaturity, I can't tell.

For while there is always the chance that my corporate fortunes will be reversed, I have glimpsed for the first time my own business mortality.[23]

It's very depressing for people to realize that their climb is over, that they have gotten as many gains as they ever will. That is especially true for those who gave the bulk of their time and emotional commitment to their work. They feel that the organization has betrayed their trust; it broke its implicit promise to continually reward hard work. Further, breaking that promise implies the organization does not value them as individuals because it has ceased to reward them.

It is a certainty that when people feel that way, their performance suffers. So does the organization. The problem is particularly acute in organizations that are not straightforward about the normalcy of the end of promotions. Organizations need to be honest about the reality that conditions have changed because you can fool some of the people some of the time, but you cannot fool many of them for long. Organizations that evade the issue create anger as well as feelings of failure in their employees. In that way they assure that productivity will decline. Many of their plateaued people quit working—but stay on the job.

Coming to terms with plateauing involves coming to terms with the realities of what we are, of our limitations, and that is not peaceful. It is a struggle in which we give up illusions. Which is *not* the same as giving up hope. Goals based on illusion are never achievable; they are carrots that dangle from the end of a stick that is attached to a band on our head. No matter how fast we run, they always remain out of reach. When we give up illusion, we suddenly see the stick that we never noticed before. Although most people first see only what they cannot do, who they will never be, and what they will not achieve, that is only the first step toward really seeing what *else* we can achieve, we can experience, we can be.

Being frustrated or feeling stuck should be the stimulus to change and grow. We are often most generative after we realize we've been stagnant. It's that realization that gives us the courage to create change and take on risks to get what we need. We make a mental transition in which we stop focusing on the past, when we think things were great, and move toward a psychological future. We do that because being stagnant, being plateaued in life, is a little death.

Most of us don't have a developmental perspective about our work. We don't think about the fact that as we climb, the nature of our successes will alter. A developmental perspective lets us see that we have to change what we require from work in order to feel satisfied. From our mid-twenties through our thirties we're in a period of full-out striving, grabbing for long-range opportunity. In the forties the windows of top opportunity open for those few who've won Olympic standing. The rest plateau; those in organizations will have no more major promotions, and self-employed professionals are in danger of becoming burned out because they're too expert in what they do. The fifties are a time of high ambition for a very few; for the majority, they are a period of acceptance.

There is a time for great dreams, and there is a time for accepting what is possible. Old expectations, which are old ambitions, are liabilities—not assets—when they are unachievable. In middle age, especially, we have to accept life's limits because that frees us from draining frustration. Paradoxically, when we accept the limits of reality, we are psychologically free to experiment and grow. Doing that, we discover capacities we weren't aware of before. The truth is the only thing that sets us free.

The Three Kinds of Plateauing

We gain a necessary perspective on what we can do to solve the problems created by plateauing when we look at the different forms that it takes. There are three kinds: *structural, content,* and *life plateauing.* While they are different from one another, they are interrelated.

Structural plateauing refers to the *end of promotions.* It is caused by an organization's hierarchy or structure. All of us know that as we climb up the familiar pyramid shape of organizations, the number of positions decreases dramatically and the opportunities to move upward decrease proportionately. But even though we know that, we hope we'll beat the odds and be one of those few who get the brass ring.

Structural plateauing is not new. What is new is that today and into the future, people will be structurally plateaued much earlier in their careers than they are prepared for. The phenomenon of structural plateauing is going to generate enormous problems in organizations for the next 15 to 25 years.

> I don't get it, I really don't. In the past five months I've had interviews for four jobs that would be promotions and I didn't get one. I thought the interviews went well. Sure, there was a lot of competition but I was a real candidate. If I wasn't, I wouldn't have gotten the interviews in the first place. What's going on?
>
> I've been in this job for six years and it's too long. It sure isn't like it used to be. For at least ten years I got promoted every two years—faster than any of the guys who came in when I did. But I worked for it—60, 70 hours a week all the time. All I did was work. Hell, all I *do* is work.
>
> I give 120 percent and it doesn't seem to be enough. This is getting to me. I know one thing though, I'm not going to give up hope.
>
> —Arnold, a 39-year-old engineer who has been in the same grade for five years

Managers, executives, and professionals who work in complex organizations are stimulated to climb the mountain because it is there and because of the intense competition among them. The visibility of the hierarchy and of the competition makes the failure to be promoted painfully obvious. Some people have great difficulty in coming to terms with structural plateauing and getting on with the rest of their lives.

People are *content plateaued* when they know their jobs *too* well. There's not enough to learn. They have become expert in their work, and they are likely to feel profoundly bored.

Marie, who is 41, has been employed as a blood bank technician in a medium-size lab for 11 years. There is no opportunity for her to become a manager; her boss is only 37. Her skills are so specialized that to change her work, she would have to make a major investment in retraining. She says:

> My current job is nice. Comfortable. But not exciting. The pay is excellent but it is not satisfying. I love work. I love meeting a deadline . . . walking away from a task that I did well. I still enjoy work. What's missing in the job is the excitement. Recognition is not enough. The work needs to change. I'm not happy with what I'm doing.

Most of us need to feel the challenge of having something unfamiliar in the task and the satisfaction that we are learning something new. We need at least a small amount of risk, which is the essence of what we call challenge.

People who are structurally plateaued frequently become content plateaued. In large organizations, structural plateauing is essentially inescapable, but content plateauing is not. The sheer size of the organization creates the possibility for job changes that do not involve promotion, but do involve new tasks and new challenges. In contrast, promotion may be insignificant to people who work in small organizations, those who are self-employed, and professionals who don't want to become managers. For them, structural plateauing is irrelevant, but content plateauing is an ever-constant danger.

People are particularly vulnerable to *plateauing in life* when work becomes the most significant sector in their lives. Work becomes the basis of their identity and self-esteem—which is fine as long as they continue to be successful. But promotions do eventually end, sometimes provoking a terrible sense of failure, and frequently mastery of the work brings feelings of tedium. When that happens, there is a good chance that they will feel *plateaued in life.*

Being plateaued in life is more profound, more total, and consequently more serious than the other forms of plateauing. From middle age on, many of us are plateaued in life. It takes courage to break out of this most difficult plateau. But unless we do, our lives will remain a faint approximation of what they might have been.

> I'm 47 and I don't know what to do. My whole life is boring. All I ever seem to do is meet my responsibilities, and I'm tired of it. Every morning I get up and go to work and come home. When I come home it's the same old routine. I read the paper, eat supper, do some work, watch television, and go to bed. Then I get up and I go to work again.
>
> I guess my life is pretty much like everybody else's, but the truth is, I'm feeling old. I'm too young to feel old! There's nothing exciting going on. Work used to be exciting. That's when I put everything into it. But now I've gone as far as I'm going to go. What am I going to do with the rest of my life? I hate the thought that it's going to be like this forever.

People who feel plateaued in life usually feel trapped; they don't know how to break out of the cycle of despair, and they are afraid to try. If they can accept the fact that they *are* plateaued and at the end of a phase, they are in a position to begin. They have the opportunity to do what they have never done, to experience what they have never felt, to become people they have not yet been. What they stand to gain is the rest of their lives.

Escaping the Trap

The fact is that *everyone* plateaus. The only difference among people is in how they handle it. The first task is always the same; it is true for individuals and it is true for organizations: *The phenomenon of plateauing must be acknowledged and the problems that it causes must be addressed.*

In itself, plateauing is not necessarily bad. In fact, since plateauing in certain aspects of our lives is inevitable, being satisfied with life while being plateaued in some parts of it is necessary for our mental well-being. But plateauing is emotionally depleting when the plateau results in the sense that work or relationships or life has no momentum. People cope and act responsibly, but there is no vitality in what they do.

While *being* plateaued is a fact, *feeling* plateaued is a psychological state. Obviously, people who feel plateaued want to experience their work and their lives differently. But how? The first step in creating psychological change is to gain insight. Thus the first purpose of this book is to explain the phenomenon of plateauing.

When we think about plateauing, we usually focus on structural plateauing, the end of promotions. The reality that promotions will end, and that they will end earlier in our careers, is a wedge that will force us to change our definition of success. Of course we will continue to esteem those who are so exceptional that they rise to the highest levels of responsibility and leadership. But the definition of success has to be broadened to include those who continue to learn and be productive at work and those who continue to mature and change in their lives. Our ideas about success have to alter so that people can feel "successful" during the whole of their lives.

But insight about a problem is only the first step. There has to be *real* change in how people live and in how organizations respond. Those changes can take place only when the phenomenon of plateauing is addressed and success is redefined. While I will provide many specific recommendations for change at work and in life, the central goals are:

> The *organization* must change its culture so that people who are structurally plateaued can continue to earn respect and experience success through mastering new challenges.
> The *manager* must be honest and supportive so that plateaued employees know where they stand and can continue to feel motivated and valued.
> The *individual* must face the issues, give up frustrating old ambitions, and take the initiative in creating new ones.

People who are plateaued have to create new opportunities by which they can gain self-esteem. Since people feel plateaued when a major commitment no longer provides satisfaction and excitement, they have to redefine what they want from the commitment, or they must take on new commitments. People need to create that feeling of movement in their inner lives, which is the only way to have a sense of future.

The truth is that I didn't really know that I was plateaued for a long time. My manager kept telling me that something would turn up and I kept getting really good performance evaluations, so I believed him. But you know, it's hard to fool yourself when guys who used to be at the same level are now three levels up and your boss is younger than you are. There were a couple of hard years there.

I finally went to my manager and said, "Let's talk," and we did. I felt better just because I took the initiative. I didn't like hearing him say that I probably wasn't going any higher, but it was a relief.

Then he asked me what I wanted, and I told him I needed a new assignment. There's no challenge any more in what I'm doing. He asked me to think about it and to come back with some specific ideas. I did, and the result was that I got to head a task force that was looking into the kinds of products that we should be developing over the next five years. I liked that, because it was a tough problem and I really got involved for the first time in years. Besides, if I wasn't really good and didn't really know the business, I'd never have been given that responsibility.

It was tough telling my wife that I'd gone about as far as I would. But her reaction was surprising. She said that she knew it was disappointing to me but, frankly, she was kind of glad because now maybe I'd take more time on the weekends so we could do things together. Between her career and mine, we'd kind of lost touch.

It's funny how it worked out, because I think I'm better off. I don't mean that I wouldn't have liked to become the general manager, I would have. But since that's not in the cards, I stopped chasing it and started doing other things instead. The result is that I do my work better than ever and I like it, but it's not the only thing I do any more. I play tennis a couple of times a week now, and I've gotten into investing. My wife and I are closer than we were, and I've got more time for friends.

It was a good ride for a long time, but then things had to change. I guess I really mean, *I* had to change. I make more money than I expected to, I've got the respect of the people I work with, and I can get new assignments that are interesting. The truth is, the quality of my life is damned good.

—Peter, age 47

2

What's the Problem?
There Are Too Many
Candidates!

Sometimes people challenge the most basic assumptions underlying this idea of plateauing. Since there are no statistics on the number of organizations experiencing increasing problems because of early plateauing, they say there is no evidence that it is a significant problem. Essentially they're saying, "You're claiming that the sky is falling down. When I look up, I see blue sky and a shining sun." When *I* look up, I see lots of storm clouds and even a few tornadoes. While I cannot cite direct data about how many people in how many organizations are increasingly troubled, the numbers that we have leave no doubt that we have many more qualified people than positions and that it's getting lots worse.

There's an old joke about a man who was asked why he was beating his donkey so mercilessly. "I'm not," he said, "I'm just trying to get his attention." That's what this chapter is intended to do—get your attention. Alas, it's mostly numbers, and some people find that about as attractive as going to the dentist. Still, the magnitude of the figures is staggering and their implications are clear: it's a new ball game. What was, is not. For many people, old ambitions, specifically for promotion, will simply not be achievable.

When I ask people where they get their expectations about what their careers will be like, they say, "From what my manager tells me," or, "From how fast I'm getting promotions compared with the people I started with."

17

We are an extraordinarily individualistic culture. We see the world in terms of *me;* how am I doing compared with everyone else? As a result of this focus on the individual, few of us pay much attention to the huge forces that determine overall rates of opportunity. Even when we know the facts we tend to discount their effect on us. We say, "I'll just work harder." Of course some people are so exceptional that they'll triumph under bleak conditions, but the vast majority are affected by the huge variables of the state of the economy and the demographic facts that determine the number of educated competitors.

When the huge variables create basically low rates of promotion opportunity, the efforts of individuals are like spitting into the wind. That's what we have now.

It is a *fact* that there are far more qualified candidates for managerial, executive, and professional positions than there are positions. That gap will continue to grow as the percentage of well-educated people continues the spectacular rise of the past decade. Some people now in their thirties—educated, ambitious, disciplined, and qualified—are facing the reality that they have already reached their ceiling.

More than any other single factor, the sheer numbers of the baby-boomers account for the unremitting competition. "A new fault line is cracking the foundation of American society. . . . The baby-boomers, grown to maturity, have finally arrived, and they are pushing for power."[2] The boomers are a gigantic bulge of 56 million people aged 26 to 40. The elite of this group are the Yuppies—extraordinarily well-educated, young urban professionals. Huge numbers of well-qualified people in their twenties and thirties are scrambling for limited job slots, creating fiery competition *within* the boomer generation, and *between* it and the older generation. And the dramatic surge of women into the labor force is compounding the pressure.

The first of the baby boom generation began reaching managerial ranks in the early 1970s. They've been reared on success stories of young people "making it" early in many fields, including management. Their expectations are high, especially those with an MBA,[62] and so is their competitiveness. The game is serious and the odds are awful. Organizations tend to play young people off against each other, so that competitiveness is continuously escalated. Caught up in a hard-driving race up the ladder in which you're either a winner or a loser and the stakes are how well you will live for the rest of your life, few are willing to come in second and no one is ready to get stuck halfway up.

While the population pressures affect all the boomers, they are most obvious among the Yuppie elite in corporate America. Some 80 percent of our young executives and professionals think their generation "faces more competition from others the same age for jobs, promotions, and the chance to get ahead" than any earlier generation. Similar conflicts are occurring in the blue-collar world as well.[2] While we have a long history of conflict between labor and management, the coming power struggle is likely to be much more intense between generations than between blue and white collars. Corporate executives in their forties and fifties are increasingly faced with ambitious, competitive, and demanding men and women in their thirties and even twenties.

What do I mean by competition? What exactly are the odds? Research at GE and other companies indicates quite consistently that back in the good old days of 1966, less than 30 percent of the people identified as leading candidates ever got the position they were shooting for. GE wondered what the odds were of making it to the executive ranks, and did a study of what had happened to managers who were evaluated as being in the top 10 percent of their peers. The company found that at age 40 the odds were 1 in 15 of making it to the top 1 percent of GE management. At age 45, the odds were 1 in 45. Nowadays the odds are even smaller.[19]

Because the competition among the baby-boomers is so intense, and because that competition will no doubt spill out to all other age groups, it is important to note that, despite all the upward mobility displayed by the high-income Yuppies, between 1979 and 1983 the annual income of people aged 25 to 34 fell *more rapidly* than the national median for all families: 14 percent decline, compared to 8.5 percent. And that 14 percent *includes* the higher-income Yuppies.[55] In addition to designer boutiques, we've had an enormous explosion in thrift shops. Among baby boomers, only 15 percent make over $30,000.[41]

While the media have paid the most attention to the elite cadre of upwardly mobile Yuppies, the basic fact is that the entire generation is *downwardly* mobile.[39] Reared in affluence, educated so they presume affluence, the Yuppies are battered by high taxes, the high cost of housing, and a lack of discretionary income despite both spouses working. Data from the Census Bureau and the Bureau of Labor Statistics show that "the real after-tax income for families headed by a person aged 25 to 34 declined 2.3 percent between 1961 and 1982"—despite the fact that the number of married women 25 to 34 who are in the labor force has risen from 29 percent to 62 percent! This means that the *combined* take-home pay of a baby-boom couple is "likely to be less [in buying power] than what each of their respective fathers alone earned at a similar age."[39] People in this situation are going to bite their competitors' jugulars with long incisors.

The effects of the demographic crush are likely to be even crueler on baby-boomer women and minorities. "Not only are there more people than ever before competing for the same positions, but there are also fewer openings on top as older workers hang on to their jobs. Moreover, this older generation of executives tends to be white and male . . . which makes it more difficult for women and minorities—an important segment of the baby boom—to get ahead. When these executives do resign, they tend to look for replacements among their own kind."[2]

While this harsh competition will affect all occupations and all professions, more attention has been paid to the coming bulge of would-be managers than any other group. Arch Patton, a former director of the management consulting firm McKinsey and Company, says that during the 1980s U.S. industry will face unprecedented personnel problems because of the aging of the baby-boom generation.

As far back as 1973 it was observed that the problem of the "accumulating management resource," as it is often referred to in management jargon ("shelf sitter" is the more colloquial term), had grown to serious proportions during the preceding two decades.[13] Observers then estimated that the number of shelf sitters in large industrial corporations was three to five times greater than it had been in the early 1950s. As corporations grew, the number of middle managers increased faster than either the worker or executive populations. Organizations developed a middle manager "belly," and competition for proportionately fewer top jobs increased significantly a decade ago. The unavoidable result was arrested career development for many thousands of middle managers. The present situation is worse, the future potentially catastrophic.

The ideal solution to this problem of intense competition for career advancement is rapid economic growth, especially organizational expansion. But most people expect that growth over the next 20 years will be slower than it has been in the past, and so they will be unremittingly competitive as they attempt to grab their share. For the baby-boomers, and for those older workers against whom they are competing, the 1980s will be a decade of scarce promotions, frustrated expectations, and job hopping. Millions of baby-boomers crowded on the first rungs of management will be forced to stay put, stuck on the ladder. Landon Y. Jones, author of *Great Expectations,* says, "A generation that had expected to be chiefs will have to be braves. . . . In effect, the entire generation will be like a large group of people being moved from a big room into a smaller room."[60] Not only will there be too little room at the top, there will be too little room in the middle.

The Measure of the Problem

Just how bad is it? That depends on the answer to three questions: (1) How many people are there in the prime working years? (2) How many people are educated? and (3) How many positions will there be in the future?

How Many People Are There?

We have had two extreme swings in our birthrate: the low point during the Depression and the high point after World War II. The Depression and the war combined to keep births very low during the 1930s and early 1940s, resulting in a relatively small number of people who are now aged 40 to 55 years old. The birthrate then soared in the years immediately after the war, peaked in 1958, and remained high until 1962.[52]

The lower birthrate in the 1930s meant that in the 1970s there were fewer people aged 35 to 45. From a high point in the 1960s, this age group, people who are now 40 to 55, lost 11 percent of its population. Since the largest number of executives fall in this age group, a critical proportion of the potential executive population was in short supply during the years 1970–1980 and *thus their promotions were rapid.*[50] Two critical points to remember: this small birth group had an unusually large number of opportunities, and their careers form the model for the expectations of today's boomers.

The number of people now aged 25 to 39 is enormous. In the ten years from 1976 to 1985, the number of people aged 30 to 39 increased to 37.4 million, a whopping 45 percent gain. In the same decade there was an even greater increase—49 percent—in those aged 35 to 39, the age bracket from which most organizations draw their next generation of top management. And the population pressure still has not peaked. From 1980 to 1990, the number of persons aged 35 to 44, the prime "middle manager" candidate group, will increase by 42 percent.[50] The Bureau of Labor Statistics projects that the labor force will grow by 29 percent between 1982 and 1995. The 45 to 54 age group, though, will expand by 48 percent, and the 35 to 44 age bracket will increase by 64 percent.[30]

The number of potential executives in this group is actually even larger than implied by these numbers because women and minority groups are now part of the potential executive population.[50] (Not only is the total number of people aged 35 to 44 much larger, but a higher percentage of people within that group are vying for managerial jobs.) The 1980 census was the first to report that slightly more than half of all women work outside the home. Today, 53 percent, or 46.7 million, American women are employed[52], up from 31.4 percent in 1950. In the baby boom group the numbers are higher: fully 67 percent of women between the ages of 18 and 34 are in the labor force.

The message is clear. Until 2004, we will have very large groups in their "best years," those between 35 and 45. As a result, until 2015 or so, when the firstborn of the baby boom will reach their mid-sixties, employers will be under heavy pressure from younger people.[17]

How Many People Are Educated?

The relatively stable and prosperous American economy of the last 30 years has produced a very educated labor force.[40] About 51 percent of all American high school graduates now go on to some form of higher education. That is an extraordinary percentage, with vast social ramifications: we are creating a nation of people with middle-class aspirations and expectations. People with college educations expect their education to enable them to live well and to do meaningful and challenging work.

Just how many people are we talking about? In 1982 there were more than 12 million enrolled in college programs, up from 9.6 million in 1973 and a 250 percent increase over 1963. We are talking about a huge number of people, with increasingly large numbers of women. Currently, the sexes are essentially equal in both undergraduate and graduate programs, with 52 percent being women.

This dramatic increase in the pool of competitors can be clearly seen in medicine, law, and business. The absolute increases in the number of degrees are extraordinary. The number of minority students alone doubled in the decade from 1970 to 1980. But the percent increases for women are simply staggering. In 1970, 699 women graduated from medical school. By 1980 the number was 3,833. That's a gain of 548 percent. By 1983-4 a third of the med students were female.[68] Even more than medicine, law has become a more female profession. Women make up nearly one-third of all lawyers under the age of 30 and about one-fourth of those under 35.[25] In 1970, 801 women graduated from law school. By 1980, that number had increased to 11,768, a jump of almost 1,500 percent! It's the same in other professions: in 1983, women got one-fourth of the doctorate degrees in science and engineering. The rise in MBAs, though, is the most important for management careers. In 1970, 1,004 women earned an MBA. Ten years later, in 1980, that figure was more than 14,000—an increase of 1,400 percent!

During the 1950s, only 56 schools offered the MBA. Most experts believe that number is now about 650.[42] In 1964 some 6,000 people earned a graduate degree in business administration. In 1976 the number increased to 30,000, with women earning 10 percent of those degrees and minorities 5 percent. In 1976 it was predicted that ten years later, in 1985, there would be 60,000 MBAs a year, with women earning 20 percent and minorities somewhat less than 5 percent.[50] Those projections were too low. By 1981 there were more than 57,000 master's degrees awarded in business, with women getting almost 25 percent. By 1983, the total number had jumped to more than 63,000.[29] In 1986, there are 71,000 graduates with MBA degrees.

The picture is actually bigger than just those graduating, and it's not just that women and minority groups are getting an education. Everyone's going to school! The total number of people engaging in some form of education is more than 46 million,[42] or one in five of our total population.

School is, of course, just the preparation for a career position. The competition in college is merely the preparation for the competition in the business world. Increasingly, women are successful competitors: they now hold 31 percent of all management jobs, up from 18 percent in 1970. Janet Norwood, Commissioner of the Bureau of Labor Statistics, runs a government agency of 2,000 people. She is one of 11,876 women who head federal, state, or local government agencies in the United States. There was not *one* such woman who claimed that distinction in the 1970 census.[59] The competing tide of managerial aspirants is further augmented by blacks and other minority members. Like women, blacks have won jobs once closed to them and have increased their proportions in almost every up-scale occupational group.[52]

The impact of this dramatic upswing in the educational level of our populace is becoming clear. ". . . Analysis of the future demand for college graduates, and of future supply, indicates that more college graduates will be available than will be needed to fill jobs that require a college degree."[65] Actually, that is misleading. The real result will be that a college degree will increasingly be required for entry into jobs that previously did not require one. One out of every five college graduates now takes a blue-collar or low salaried job.[2] The value of the degree will be less, but the need for one will be higher.

Even MBAs are being affected. As companies began to streamline their operations and employment levels in the wake of the recent recession, they reduced the number of MBAs hired. Xerox, for example, routinely hired 75 to 100 MBAs in the early 1980s. In 1984 that number was cut in half. Though the signs are mixed and the outlook far from uniformly dismal, business school experts believe that the phenomenal production of MBAs during the last two decades may have created a glut in the market. Wharton officials, for example, are warning that some MBA schools and their graduates may soon face lean times. Wharton dean Russell E. Palmer says, "The MBA market went too far, too fast. Something's got to happen."[42]

Once largely reserved for educated, upper- and middle-class white males, available management and professional positions are progressively being thrown open to a much larger and heterogenous group of candidates.[62]

The increased size of this pool of educated people is creating unremitting competition and this competition will continue in the coming decades.

How Many Positions Will There Be?

By the dawn of the 1990s, there will be up to twice as many trained managers, administrators, professionals, and high technologists in the United States as there will be a genuine need for.

Even a very large number of educated and qualified people does not necessarily create problems. Problems exist when the number of available positions is significantly less than the number of appropriate applicants. In the coming decade, the number of people aged 35 to 44, the prime middle-management candidate group, will increase 42 percent. The Labor Department projects that the number of professional and technical workers will increase by 30 percent from 1980 to 1990. Meanwhile, the Bureau of Labor Statistics projects the number of *jobs* for managers will increase only 19.1 percent.[65] Economist Anthony Carnevale says that in a few years, by 1990, we will have an additional 10.4 million people who are trying to get into middle management. But we will have achieved only 1.7 million new management jobs.[70] Between 1970 and 1980 there was a 24 percent expansion of management jobs. There was, however, a *48 percent* expansion in the number of qualified people. With the dramatic increase in undergraduate and graduate business degrees, that kind of disparity can only get worse.

While there will be significant problems in the professions—too many physicians, lawyers, accountants, and so on—the problem in the 1980s that has been written about the most is overcrowding in management.

The New York Stock Exchange lists 1,528 companies; the American Exchange lists 900, and there are probably another 2,000 large unlisted companies—approximately 4,500 in total. In big companies the number of managers earning $100,000 and more is estimated at about 100 per company; in small companies the list runs much shorter, possibly a dozen. Even allowing for a generous average of 80 highly paid officials in each of 4,500 companies, that means a top managerial group of only 360,000 nationwide.[20]

With only 360,000 top-level jobs, there simply aren't that many top-management or even higher-middle-management jobs available. To make matters worse, advances in technology have further eliminated many support-type jobs in the $20,000 to $50,000 range.[20] Experts say that desktop computers and office automation will make middle managers more efficient and eliminate the need for many of them. If fast-growing new-technology industries were to create huge numbers of management positions within their own companies, the problem might be ameliorated. But such companies need technical specialists and computer experts, not additional managers.

The severe recession of 1981–1982 also made jobs harder to come by, especially because many companies cut management staff. Well into the recovery, they have not gone back to their prerecession levels. The cutback is not simply a short-term response to the recession. It is likely to continue, because we no longer dominate world markets and foreign competition is not expected to lessen. Most organizations are now cautious about increasing costs, so only a relative few will expand swiftly and largely. Now, and into the future, the number of positions in the middle and the top of organizations will be much less than the number of appropriate candidates for those jobs.

Because governments, schools, universities, hospitals, and other kinds of organizations are not expanding, it is toward industry—both manufacturing and service—that we will look for the jobs needed to absorb our population increase. Our economy has never before been asked to provide *new* jobs for 26 percent more 30–34-year-olds in a five-year period or for 45 percent more 30–39-year-olds in a decade. The closest approximation to this massive need for new employment occurred during the demobilization of the military in the mid-1940s. But even so, total employment increased barely 11 percent from 1945 to 1950, and only 25 percent from 1945 to 1955.[50]

From 1945 to 1955, there was an enormous, war-created demand for every kind of manufacturing and service product, and this resulted in a growing economy and expanding organizations. Quite the opposite condition exists today: the economy is shakily recovering from the recession of 1981–1982. That recession was the deepest in the postwar era and tied for the longest. It set post-Depression records in farm and home mortgage foreclosures, business bankruptcies, bank failures, and unemployment levels.

Inflation is better today, running at a third of the 13 percent rate during the Carter Administration. But *real* interest rates—market figures minus inflation—are as high or higher than they were in January 1981. Now, "the enormous deficits stretching out to the end of the 1980s will make it difficult either to increase spending programs or ease money and credit as anti-recession therapies."[36] The boom is over.

These basic economic trends affect everyone. The long postwar history of rising real standards of living has come to an end. The last recession got our attention! It may be a decade or more before healthy new capital investments can spur productivity enough to renew the great expectations from the past.[55] For most organizations, the 1981–1982 recession altered the mood from buoyant expansion to caution. Most institutions are simply not expanding much, if at all: governments are cutting back, schools and universities are retrenching, hospitals are not expanding, and most corporations are not increasing the number of their managers and executives. As a matter of fact, many are cutting back.

Cuts in Middle Management

Competition can be keen when organizations are not expanding as fast as the growth of the pool of people. Competition is keener still when the population is increasing but organizations are not expanding at all. Competition is keenest when organizations cut back in size.

In previous recessions, middle-aged managers watched, or ordered, layoffs of blue-collar workers or younger, salaried coworkers, but they themselves were largely spared. Companies retained longtime salaried staff out of "loyalty"—they didn't want a reputation for dumping people. So there was real security in many firms. But that changed as the recession made the fact of worldwide competition frighteningly clear and permanent. As a result, many firms cut out layers of management and combined jobs. What was once rare became commonplace: middle managers in their forties and fifties were—and are—being forced out.[69]

Economists and job counselors estimate that the number of managers in their mid-forties to late fifties who have been dismissed in recent years has grown to record levels, in the *tens of thousands*. *Business Week* reports that 40 percent of our top, 1,200 corporations cut middle management in 1982, and in half of them, the cuts were major. In 1982, salaried staff cuts between 10 and 25 percent were being imposed at General Motors, Acme-Cleveland Corporation, National Semiconductor, and scores of other companies in numerous industries.[69],[53] The same phenomenon is reported internationally: middle-management slots were cut 15 percent between 1980 and 1982 worldwide.[39]

The cutbacks in management did not end during the recent recession. In August 1984, GM announced that the following November it would begin eliminating "redundant" positions in its roughly 120,000-member white-collar work force. They will reassign some of the affected employees and force others to retire early. And, unable to slash its wages to Japanese levels, GM is pushing to computerize auto manufacturing.[35] With so much busywork being done by computers, fewer employees would be needed in traditional categories. When asked, GM officials say they can't estimate the possible effect on employment but "the handwriting is on the wall," as a technical center manager puts it. Some experts expect the ax to fall hardest on GM's salaried ranks. "Job obsolescence will affect the white-collar worker much worse than the blue-collar worker, and that's a fact!"[22] If the computerization succeeds, GM will undoubtedly be copied by many other manufacturers.

When there's a need to make meaningful cost reductions, the people who are cut tend to be higher-paid; they also tend to be older. Middle management grew hugely in the past three decades. We got carried away with managers. Now, it's back to lean times.

It's not news when companies cut the ranks of management when things are tough. So it was not surprising that there were cutbacks in management in the last recession. What *is* news is that the cuts are continuing today, while the economy is recovering. Eugene Jennings of Michigan State University has found that 89 of the 100 largest U.S. companies have continued to make cuts since 1980.

The management reductions are hitting every kind of business—service as well as manufacturing. In an article published in September 1985, *Business Week* reported that in the preceding month significant reductions were made in AT&T, Ford, Union Carbide, and CBS. In 1986, AT&T's Information Services will cut 24,000 jobs, and 8,000 of them will be white-collar positions. Over the next five years, Ford North American Automotive Division will reduce management by 20 percent, or 9,600 jobs. Downsizing is occurring at Eastman Kodak, General Electric, Apple Computer, United Technologies' subsidiary Mostek, Du Pont, Lever Brothers, U.S. Steel, and Polaroid—and these are only a sample.[26]

The Horizon

Our national resource, which is also our national problem, is an almost unbelievably large number of educated, motivated, and competitive people striving to achieve both traditional and nontraditional kinds of success. Traditionally, they want increasing amounts of responsibility, money, power, status—all the things that come with promotion. Nontraditionally, they also want their work to expand their minds, fulfill their souls, and encourage their personal growth—all the things that come from unending challenge.

Unfortunately, there aren't all that many such jobs around; and, as the numbers show, it's not going to get much better.

We know that most of the new jobs that have been created in the last decade have come from new startup companies. Many hope that the baby-boomers will find their place in the sun in those organizations. And they *are* likely to find jobs there, but it is improbable that all or even most of the companies will succeed and become the next IBM. And, in any event, large and successful high-tech companies also follow the Golden Rule of 99%, which dictates room at the top for only 1 percent. The chances of everybody finding endless fulfillment of traditional and nontraditional gratifications in the workplace seem to me not just slim, but downright skinny.

Hey, everybody, the sky *is* falling!

3

Structural Plateauing—
It's *Not* the
Peter Principle

When people ask me what I'm currently working on, and I tell them plateauing, it's not unusual for their faces to go blank for a moment as they try to figure out what that means. Then their eyes light up as they make the connection and they say, "Oh, yes! The Peter Principle!"

That is totally wrong. Today, plateauing and the Peter Principle are the reverse of each other. Plateauing is a condition in which many able people will be unable to rise to levels in which they would be competent. The Peter Principle is a condition in which people rise to levels in which they are *in*competent.

In the boom years of the 1950s, 1960s and 1970s, when the low birthrate of the Depression resulted in a small labor force, we had the largest number of opportunities in our history for our smallest birth group. Those conditions gave rise to the book called *The Peter Principle*, published in 1969, in the midst of that boom period.[51] During those years, organizations expanded so swiftly that promotions were unusually rapid. The result was that sometimes people were promoted even though they lacked sufficient experience. Without adequate grounding in their field, often without personal maturity, they were unprepared to cope with large responsibilities and major decisions.

For two and a half decades, people were promoted as fast as possible (some faster than they should have been) because of the demand for executive talent. Industry, local, state, and federal governments, schools, colleges and universities, and hospitals were expanding so greatly that they all competed vigorously for managerial talent, which was scarce. Today, no major sector in society is in a phase of exuberant growth—not industry, schools, hospitals, or governments.

In addition to the sheer increase in size, organizations were becoming more complex, thus creating high-level jobs. Managers had to learn and apply new knowledge related to advancing technology, changing dynamics in the marketplace, a better use of human resources, protection of the environment, and increased government legislation. As business became more international, these tasks became even more complex.[28]

As a result, specialties emerged within management: strategic planners, computer specialists, financial analysts, manufacturing control systems specialists, equal opportunity officers, and the like. And, as corporations grew larger, they brought in-house many activities that had previously been performed by outside service groups. That included lawyers, human resource specialists, money managers, computer programmers, communication specialists, and others. Those were now new departments, and they opened many new managerial spots. These specialties also permitted younger people with advanced degrees to leapfrog to senior positions.

In 1945, the 25 largest corporations in the United States had an average of 6 vice-presidents. In 1965, each averaged 16 vice presidents, some of whom were in charge of functions like community affairs, taxes, public relations, and government relations, jobs that 20 years before either hadn't existed or had been relatively low-level.[50]

All this means that we went through a period of very rapid organizational growth in which there was a disproportionate expansion of white-collar and middle-management jobs. The shape of the organizational pyramid changed as middle management grew exceptionally quickly, and promotions were swift as long as those functions kept expanding.[62] Many middle managers, therefore, enjoyed a long period of swift mobility, and extraordinary numbers who rose in the 1960s ended up competing for the top.[67]

Those very unusual conditions of rapid promotion continued

long enough that they came to be seen as normal. For a whole generation, promotion became *the* organizational reward for performance. Many people concentrated on how they would get the next upward move—even as they were just settling in to their most recent promotion.[45]

Too-swift promotions and the Peter Principle are yesterday's problem. Today our problem is *underpromotion.* The thing to remember about baby-boom and education statistics is they can't be wished away. They're not projections into the future; those are the number of people who are *already* born, educated, and in the labor force. Many people are already overexperienced and over-qualified, staying at the same level and even in the same job for too long. Those ranks will grow larger and larger.

The vernacular plateauing phrases—"out to pasture," "a slug," "peaked," "shelf sitter," "over the hill," "burned out"— imply that the Peter Principle is operating. That losers plateau because they've reached incompetence. That plateaued people can't hack it where they are and they just hang in there, like dead wood or an empty suit, taking up space, going through the motions.

Since the Peter Principle is well known and the words are a common part of the corporate culture, everyone including the people who are plateaued, knows them. It's hard for plateaued people to avoid wondering if that's how others see them. Even harsher, it is hard for plateaued people to avoid thinking of themselves in these terms. While many plateaued people are consciously certain that they're doing a good job and could handle a higher one, these descriptions and the heavy judgment they carry often create a nagging uncertainty about whether they've reached their limits. "Could it be that I'm on the shelf? Out to pasture? Does anyone else know? I don't like thinking about this stuff." It's hard to remain confident if you're a member of a group that everyone talks about, and thinks of, and responds to, as losers.

In any organization there are stars, solid citizens, and losers. The danger of the plateauing stereotype, the Peter Principle portrait, is that it describes solid citizens as losers. Then previously productive people stop being productive mostly because they feel taken for granted, ignored, sidelined. When people are treated like losers—when others avoid their company, stop giving them important assignments, no longer ask their opinion—they become losers. They become people who quit, only they continue to hang around.

When plateaued people are *not* made to suffer the slings and arrows of outrageous judgment, they remain productive and motivated. Because they are respected, they respect themselves. We need to make the very different assumption that plateaued people *are* competent and productive, are in fact the critical core of the white-collar labor force. While the Peter Principle does describe some individuals, the essential reality is that plateauing is a normal stage in everyone's career. Plateauing is caused by competition—and don't ask for whom that bell tolls; it rings for virtually everyone. Of course there's always some truth to the Peter Principle. Organizations will always make some errors and promote some people they shouldn't. But today, it's more likely that almost everyone who reaches the rungs of middle management could perform well at least at the next higher level. But, for many, that opportunity will not occur.

A Case (or Two) in Point

Ron, who has a PhD in engineering and an MBA, has worked for a Fortune 100 company for twenty years. For the last seven, he's been the chief of engineering for a very successful division. In the division there are six other people at his rank; above them, there's a general manager. Now 45, he earns enough money that pursuing more money for its own sake isn't very important to him. What is important, what drives him, is his desire to become the general manager. He wants that promotion as a corporate acknowledgment that he's as good as he thinks he is, and more simply because it's the next rung on his ladder upward. He knows that if he doesn't make it soon, the window of promotability is going to be slammed shut. If he doesn't get that promotion quickly, the chances are that he won't get any, any more. The race will be over.

> I have to say the company has treated me well and it's a good place to work. But I don't understand what's going on. When I compare myself with the others at my level, I'm convinced that I'm the most qualified to be the general manager. The last three general managers were brought in from outside the division so it's like we're a training ground for people who are going up in the corporation. None of us here on staff level has had a promotion for years. We're always one of the top four divisions in the whole company in terms of profit so we

must be doing something right. So why don't we get the recognition that we've earned? Why haven't I gotten the recognition that I deserve?

In the last four or five years I've found myself thinking about leaving. I'm pretty confident that I'm damn salable, but sometimes I'm not so sure. I know that if I'm going to do it, I better hurry because at 50 I won't look young any more. But it's hard to leave after so many years and I'm not sure that there's anything better out there. Sometimes I think I really want to get out of the corporate bureaucracy and invent something in my garage. But I'd miss all the resources I have here.

Both of the past general managers said they've tried to do something for me. They called people in other divisions but nothing happened. Everyone tells me I'm general-manager material but after being passed over a couple of times, I have to ask myself if other people perceive me the same way I see myself.

I've been at the same grade level for nine years and I'm at the top of the pay scale so my raises aren't very big any more. The money doesn't feel important but I need something. The truth is that I need that promotion because there's nowhere else to go. If I don't get it, I don't know what else to do.

I asked people in the division what they thought of Ron, and everyone agreed that he was far and away the brightest and most gifted of the senior people. Everyone also agreed that he had more potential than was being used and that was a pity. But everyone also agreed that the people who had been brought in as general managers had an edge; they were just a little more able.

Ron is in the top level of middle management. Even there, below the executive level, slots are few and openings are scarce. As outstanding as he is, in that competition there are some who are better. He is certainly able to handle more responsibility, but if he stays in that company, he faces 20 more years at the same grade. Objectively, he's done well. But as good a race as he ran, he is plateaued. Poignantly, as successful as he is, he is not happy. Worse, he is unhappy. His vivid successes were in the past. In a world where "success" requires ever-expanding responsibilities, more money, higher status, and increasing recognition, past triumphs are not enough to cushion his feeling of deadness, since it looks like there won't be any more.

People plateau for two primary reasons. One is that they are not good enough to be promoted to higher or different responsibilities. Sometimes, as in technical fields, their skills are no longer current. Often, though they are excellent at what they currently do, they are not talented in terms of the next set of responsibilities. Those usually involve managing people; the transition from technical expert to manager is a common stopping place.

The second and most important reason why people plateau is that there is simply nowhere for them to go. Even on extraordinary people, the ceiling of the organization presses down; there is no place to go up. In this sense, success creates limits. As people ride upward, eventually they attain a place where positions are so few that promotions virtually end. That even happens to people who are brilliant.

Daniel was the executive financial vice president of a major corporation in 1975, at the age of 35. Plateaued, he moved to an even larger firm when he was 40, again to chief financial officer. While he is extraordinary in that role, he's certain that as a money man he'll never become the president; in this company all the presidents have been engineers who served as division presidents. Shackled by the platinum fetters of stock options and other executive perks so that he feels he cannot leave, at the age of 45 he's bumped against his ceiling. There are no more buttons on his "up" elevator.

Of course most people who plateau are not as outstanding or as successful as Daniel or Ron. Most people are sturdily competent, and they plateau below the executive level because there are lots of competent and experienced people in all organizations. And there's not enough room to promote them all.

Today, few people plateau because they've reached their limits. Instead, promotions end, despite the ability to cope with greater responsibilities, simply because *there's no place to move people up.* Now the truth is that most people know the organizational chart and understand it in their head. Unfortunately, many people have an interior shelf somewhere around their neck so that information from their head does not reach their belly, where passion lives. Understanding the organizational pyramid does not always mean that people emotionally accept its consequences. Many people who have been successful don't accept the inexorable end of promotion because, for decades, that goal has been their entire future.

The Organizational Pyramid: Basis of Structural Plateauing

You will recall from Chapter 1 that I define three types of plateauing: structural, content, and life. The first probably could have been named "career plateauing," but I prefer the term "structural" because the fundamental cause of the slowing rate of progress and the inevitable end of promotions is the pyramid shape, the structure, of most organizations.

Structural plateauing means that promotions have ended. Of course people may experience temporary plateauing several times in their career, but ultimately it will be a permanent state. As long as they remain in that organization, though their job may change, there will be no significant increases in their responsibilities, status, money, or power. At best, any future moves will be horizontal; demotion is a possibility.

There are several key ideas to keep in mind about structural plateauing:

It is inevitable.
It happens to everyone.
It is a normal phase in every career.
It is already occurring at younger and younger ages.
It is caused by the organization's structure.
Its rate is determined by huge and impersonal demographic and economic factors that no individual can change.
It is a normal phenomenon and, as such, it is emotionally neutral.
It generates significant problems only when promotion is the overwhelmingly important motivator in an organization and in an individual's life.

The Rule of 99%

In every large and complex organization, the number of positions at the highest decision-making level is always less than 1 percent of the number of employees. Although it is true that some people who are executives but not at the top are frustrated, I've arbitrarily set the top 1 percent as not plateaued. If only 1 percent will not plateau, 99 percent will. I call that the Rule of 99%. (see Figure 1). It's the reason promotions end long before retirement for essentially everyone. The rule of 99% dictates that becoming structurally plateaued is virtually inevitable. It is normal. It should be anticipated. The only difference among people is how long it takes them to get there.

Of 100 people who are hired because they have all the right qualities and look outstanding, only 10 will reach any level of middle management and only 1 will reach the executive level. Despite intelligence, ambition, effort, and motivation, and even though you're in your mental prime, in the end it's a numbers game.

IBM, for example, has 383,000 employees. There are 44,000 managers; within that group, 6,000 are considered middle man-

Figure 1. The Rule of 99%. Less than 1 percent of managers make it to the top of an organization.

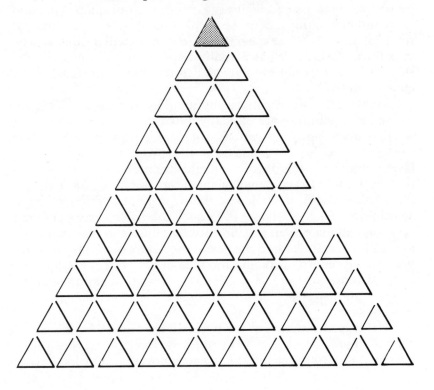

agement. Approximately 1,400 positions are considered to be in the executive ranks, and there are always five people in readiness for each one of those jobs. Actually, the core leadership is made up of fewer than 50 people. That's a typical organizational pyramid— a huge base, a fair middle, and a little pimple on the top.

There is an awful inconsistency between the myth and the reality of work, between the basic cause of plateauing and the false assumption that people plateau because they lost what they had or, worse, never had it. The Horatio Alger myth says that if you work really hard and well, there's no ceiling on where you can go. That's just not true. In every organization there are limits on the span of control; increasing amounts of power go to decreasing numbers of people. The slopes of the pyramid become steeper the higher up you look.

The Triangle Is Not Smooth

People think the pyramid has smooth sides, like the triangles in high school trig books. That's not so. The organizational pyramid looks more like a ziggurat, a tower with dramatic indentations and inclinations. Because people imagine the organizational slopes as smooth, they expect their promotions will decline slowly, in a linear fashion. What actually happens is that, because the slopes of the pyramid are irregular, promotion opportunities decline abruptly.

Think of the organizational pyramid as composed of layers in which responsibilities are basically different. The base, the largest level, is made up of operations, the people who actually do the work. The next level is made up of those who implement the top layer's decisions; this involves tactical management. The executive level does strategic management, creating the objectives for the organization as a whole and the strategies by which they will be achieved. Each level does different work and has very different decision-making power. It is immensely difficult to move from the top grade of one layer into the next if the nature of the responsibilities expands enormously and the type of power changes intrinsically. At those junctures, the organization contracts very sharply, as fewer and fewer people are allowed to make increasingly large decisions.

The jagged contours of the pyramid are created by the vastly different numbers of people at different levels of responsibility. Executives are responsible for basic innovation and long-range decisions. The Rule of 99% results from the fact that executive decisions are fundamentally different from those of management and only a few members of an organization can have the power to make them.

A drawing of the organizational pyramid will make this clear. Figure 2 is a chart of the administrative slots in the field and at headquarters in each rank of the FBI. The shape of the organization is typical.

It's obvious that the base of a pyramid, let's say the lower third, contains many more people than the midsection or the top. As you enter the ranks of management, there are lots of positions in the lower third of the management pyramid. The sheer number of jobs allows for a great deal of mobility, both lateral and upward. It is not uncommon for people to change positions every 18 to 24 months in the organizational base, during the first decade of a career. In addition, during that first decade, people who look especially promising tend to receive a great deal of training and attention. That combination of frequent job changes and high level of attention creates certain expectations. People assume they'll continue to get attention and their jobs will continue to change often. In fact, frequent job change becomes an important form of attention, a sign of being successful.

Figure 2.   A typical organizational pyramid.

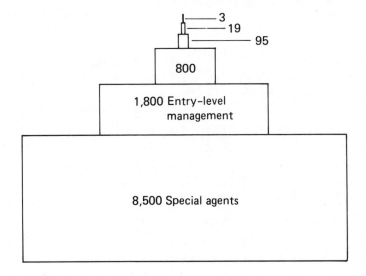

However, that frequency of job change and the rate of promotion must decline when people move up beyond the base. Even lateral moves become less common because there are far fewer positions. At the same time, people's jobs become more complicated and they become increasingly expert in their work. It is easy to move entry-level people around because they're inexperienced and therefore largely interchangeable. But experts and experienced managers are less interchangeable, so they remain in their positions far longer. It is easy for people to experience that as a decline in the organization's interest in them, as the decline of significant rewards. Ultimately, the slowdown or lack of even lateral mobility can be experienced as a punishment, the fate of the invisible person.

Tougher at the Top

There is another consequence of the pyramid shape: the farther up you go, the harder it gets. There are many people in the base, so there is a relatively wide distribution of ability at the beginning. Upward mobility is very competitive, so those who are less able don't climb. The result is that the higher up you go, the more equal people become, because only those who are outstanding have been promoted to higher levels. See Figure 3.

Figure 3.   The breadth of ability.

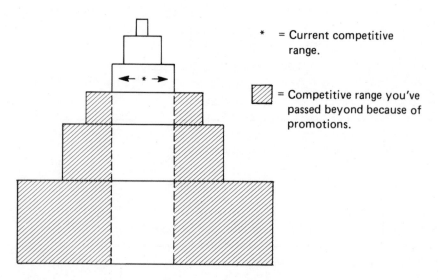

Promotion is competitive. In order to be promoted you have to look better than your competitors. As your peers narrow to those who are exceptional, it gets harder and harder to stand out. As you ascend from the middle ranks up, your rate of performance has to increase in larger and larger increments in order to be average. The rate of improvement that used to be enough to get you promoted, now may not even keep you in place. In the higher ranks, the rate of improvement has to increase exponentially, and so does the effort required to achieve it.

> At the level I'm at, I'm beginning to have to ask myself how high I want to go. It was really important to me to be promoted to engineering manager. When I started out I was responsible for two people. Now I've got a whole project under me. My next promotion would involve a whole section, usually three to five projects. That's coming up in a year or two. But I'm not sure I want to go any higher than that. I can already see that work is taking up more and more of my time, but it's not enough just to do a good job. If I want to get promoted I have to do something that people will remember, some kind of high energy thing. It's not just engineering now, it's also politics. I like engineering better.

Organizations with Major Plateauing Problems

Plateauing shows up as a major problem most often in mature, large organizations that run a tight race, reward the winners significantly, and create a very confined system in which promotion is the only important reward. Such an organization has created a major problem for itself. The Rule of 99% says that promotions will end. Eventually some of the best people will become frustrated and ineffective, which in the long run harms the organization as much as the individuals.

Michael is a 39-year-old engineer who has been in the same grade for five years. For the first decade of his career, he was promoted about every two years. Now he says:

> This is a good company and I have to be reasonable and say that it's been pretty good to me. But I earned that. I still work damn hard. Right now it bothers me

that even though my assignments get bigger and I'm putting in even more time, my grade doesn't change. Without a promotion, I'm not really sure what they think of me even though my manager keeps telling me I'm terrific. I'm tired of nice words. Now let them show me.

People who work in complex organizations are forced to face the issue of plateauing because the hierarchy of the organization, in itself, creates the motive to move up. People want to climb that mountain simply because it's there. In addition, the competition to climb, the sheer visibility of the race, increases people's drive to be one of the winners. When there is a formal hierarchy, it's easy to know who is still climbing, who is stuck, and who is falling. The failure to be promoted becomes obvious. That can generate so much pain that people can't come to terms with it.

At 59, Craig is a middle manager in a technical division of one of our largest corporations. He's been in the same grade for 19 years and in the same job for 14. Nonetheless, when I asked him if he expected any more promotions, he said:

> After 19 years with no grade promotion, and at my age, I know my options are getting smaller. But my ambition never moderated! I guess I recognize the situation, but don't really accept it. I can still get mad and sad, and that coexists with rational control. People who worked for me are now my bosses. I don't expect further promotions, but that would make me happy. I don't think I'm up for general manager, but maybe I'm wrong. I haven't given up. I don't intend to. That would be fatal—acknowledging there's no hope, no future. I don't want to feel sorry for myself and I don't want sympathy. I certainly hoped for more and I still do. I'm not bitter and I don't harbor ill feelings. But I don't understand it.

In addition to the impersonal reasons for structural plateauing, of course there are personal ones. Some people are just not hell-bent on achieving increasing amounts of traditional success. When they arrive at a comfortable standard of living and work they find interesting, they don't want bigger responsibilities. And, even in organizations that have hired the brightest, a very few will be brighter than the rest. Those who are specialists, and whose expertise is not central to the main business of that organization, will plateau early because they are unlikely to be selected for general management. In addition, organizations need different kinds of leadership at different times. "Some people are better at starting things up, some are better at squeezing the most out of them once they are running, and some are better at fixing them when they go wrong."[21]

When organizational circumstances change, people can become more or less valuable than they were. Then opportunities may be created for some who had been plateaued, and others may suddenly find themselves on the sidelines.

Promotion possibilities are critically influenced by the life phase of the organization. Between 1969 and 1974, a period when the economy was good, the average increase in the number of jobs for mature companies was 1 percent. Young, innovative, high-tech organizations, on the other hand, created a 40.7 percent increase in new jobs.[46]

As organizational cycles change, plateauing problems increase. The most obvious case is when a period of expansion ends and is followed by a stable phase. A worse case is when the next phase is one of contraction. In that case, naturally, structural plateauing will occur earlier in people's careers, and to more people, than it did in the growth phase. More complex problems are created if a stable phase is followed by a period of limited growth with limited promotion opportunities; a choice must then be made between younger, ambitious employees with promise and older, experienced employees who had been plateaued.

Plateauing is more of a problem in organizations that recruited the most competitive, ambitious, and able people than it is with those who hired people not quite so outstanding or ambitious. Competition increases competitiveness.

When I wrote the draft of my first paper on plateauing, I sent it to 15 executives I knew and asked them to tell me what sounded right and what seemed wrong. Thirteen of them said that the paper was right on the mark. The other two said, "What problem?" I had to think about that for a while. When I looked at the kinds of corporations that agreed with me that plateauing was a major problem and those that didn't, it became clear. The 13 executives who agreed with me were from organizations like IBM. The two vice presidents who said, in the politest way, that I was crying wolf were at a large life insurance company and AT&T.

Some 15 or 20 years before I wrote that paper, the time when most of their managers would have been hired, the really terrific graduates would have gone to the fast-track organizations of the time: IBM, Polaroid, Xerox, and the like. They would never have gone to work for a life insurance company or the old AT&T—they could just as well have gone into the postal service. The reason those two vice presidents could honestly claim that structural plateauing was not a big issue was that in those organizations, it wasn't. Most of the people who worked for them were more motivated by security than ambition.

Structural plateauing is a more important problem in organizations that hire exceptional people, are internally competitive, reward success significantly, make a long-term commitment to their employees as individuals, and have a policy of not firing experienced people. IBM is a perfect example.

Changing Circumstances

Promotions were not always so important. I was born in 1933, deep in the Depression, and I remember when success meant survival. When I was a child, all my father asked from work was that it allow him to support his family. He had no other requirements. My father's agenda was keeping wolves from the door and since he did it, he felt good about himself.

We who are middle-class and educated have very different requirements from work in order for us to be satisfied. Affluent enough that survival is not an issue, we want our work to give us opportunities to feel that we are learning, stretching, extending. Our work forms a large part of our identity, and we want work to allow us feelings of pride. But much of that pride is based on being a winner—which means being promoted.

The baby-boomers have all these requirements of work, and they will push to make their careers as good as the group before them. Accustomed to having to shove and compete, they will push even harder as their expectations are affected by changing circumstances, especially the past recession.

"If economics is one factor that has created a feeling of downward mobility, demographics is another. There are, quite simply, too many people in the same cohort [10-year age group]. An MA, MD, or MBA means so much less now because there are so many more of them. In almost every occupation, the competition is up and the rate of promotion down for the baby-boom generation. . . .

It doesn't just seem that way—the highway to the Hamptons really is more crowded."[60]

Expectations of success will not be met for long or for many, as long as success is defined largely by promotion. The combination of a very large, educated, qualified, and ambitious population, and a long period of cautious organizational expansion, has an inexorable result: promotion will be a scarce reward, even for outstanding performance, at least in the upper two-thirds of most organizations.

Structural plateauing has always been a fact in careers. Now it is occurring earlier, and to more people. In the late 1970s, the average age at which managers plateaued was 47. Today, it is probably closer to 42. And some truly able people in their early thirties are already plateaued in certain industries like banking and insurance. As people continue to focus on promotion and work for it and expect it, the possibility of widespread disappointment, disillusionment, and feeling of failure is high. Few people have really thought through the inevitable consequences of the economic and population facts.

The baby-boomers grew up in affluence but became adults during hard times. Their expectations were created by good years and their competitiveness by bad years. They represent an organizational time bomb—they insist upon the success of promotion and most organizations will not be able to meet their demands. Or, if their demands are met, those in their forties and fifties will be shelved and alienated. Decreasing rewards and scarcer promotions are creating the probability of more conflict between generations than we have ever had.

Stephen Hardis, vice chairman of Eaton Corporation, described the situation to me this way:

> A key element in this problem is the generational problems within corporations. Most of today's senior managers came out of the experience of the Depression and World War II with a profound sense of gratitude to the corporation for being provided a job that ultimately gave them a far more prosperous standard of living than they had ever envisioned. These managers genuinely believe in the corporation. They bitterly resent the lack of similar commitment of today's younger managers.
>
> Today's manager, in contrast, grew up in a period of unparalleled economic prosperity and tends to compare

his lot in life with peers who have started their own corporations, have gone into investment banking, law firms, consulting, etc. They are unhappy with some of the constraints imposed by the corporate organizational modes and uncertain that they can really achieve the same kind of prosperity and control of their lives that they would have if they had gone into self-employment.[27]

The solution is to redefine success. When people persist in wanting what they cannot get, frustration is high and satisfaction and productivity are low. Even worse, creativity is lost, for both the individual and the organization. People have to accept the inevitability of structural plateauing and redirect their ambition.

Promotion is simply not forever.

In an enlightened corporate culture, we must help people reach a point where their professionalism is the essential source of their pride, their sense of growth, their feeling of achievement. They have to perceive "success" as using their abilities, meeting challenges, continuing to learn, and making a contribution. Then they can feel fulfilled in the present and anticipate the future as exciting.

4

Promotion:
The Psychological
Bottom Line

Not everyone is distressed when promotions end. Some people
don't want larger responsibilities, don't want to play the political
games of higher status, don't want to compete any more, and don't
want to work any harder than they already are. They are, or
ultimately become, satisfied with the work they do and their level
of achievement. In the best of circumstances, they don't want to be
promoted because they're happy with how they're living; they've
achieved a quality of life that satisfies them.

Structural plateauing does not, in other words, have to create
gut-wrenching problems. But if often does. For one thing, it means
the end of the realistic goodies, those marvelous gains in respect,
authority, money, and perks that result from promotion. That's
disappointing, of course, but it's not tragic. What, then, accounts
for the real despair that so many experience when promotions
stop? Such despair is not explained simply by the end of further
objective gains. More dynamic pain is involved, griefs closer to the
sense of one's core self.

Promotion and Self-Worth

An organization can reward good work in lots of ways, but promotion is the most valued. Unlike verbal praise or a symbolic pat on

the head, it's a put-up or shut-up response: either you get it or you don't. It's also the only reward that can affect the organization. It's the essence of recognition and affirmation because it results in more power. As you rise higher and higher, promotion is *in reality* the response that says, "You're really good. In fact, you're so good that we'll let you make bigger decisions that involve more money and more people. You're so good that we'll let you get involved in strategy and policy. We've watched you and assessed you, and you belong with us. You're in the club."

The promise of someday being in the club is a big carrot. Whether it's a move upward in a complex hierarchy or the promotion to partnership in a professional organization, the desire to be on a par with your superiors is a powerful motive. In the area of life where we give the most and try the hardest, being accepted as an equal of those who were once superiors is an achievement of immense emotional weight.

Howard is the area general manager for a division of a financial services firm. Now 48, he realizes that in this position even though his talents as a salesman still stand him in good stead, he's reached his top spot. In the last few years he's been trying to come to terms with the fact that he's plateaued. More than anything, he'd like a promotion to corporate headquarters. I asked him why he needed a promotion.

> I evaluate myself against all the people who have those other, higher jobs. It's me against them. When I'm not chosen, I want to know in what way they are better than me. Only a promotion counts; all other forms of praise are easy. I want to see that the higher-ups really believe that in some ways, I'm as good as the rest.
>
> Anything else isn't satisfying. That promotion means I'd be in a different club. I'm not sure what being in that other pond would bring me because I haven't been there . . . deference, yes, there would be deference and I like that. I want the opportunity to increase my leverage on affairs. The affirmation I want is to carry more weight. And I could do that just as well as the guys who are there. If I don't get one of those big jobs that means someone else is preferred over me.

Promotion is a judgment that usually involves the core of how we feel about ourselves. When it is offered, our image of our core self is confirmed. When it is available and we are *not* chosen, our perception of our core self can be threatened.

Most Americans tend to identify with work. Work is not what we *do*, it is what we *are*. In our guts, we are what we do. The rejection of being passed over for promotion can be experienced as the rejection of our total self. The people who feel worst are those who cannot limit the implied criticism of being passed over, who cannot say to themselves, "I am not as good in *work* as I thought I was." What's on the line is the total sense of self-esteem, of value as a person. When something shakes our essential sense of identity and worth, we feel anxious and depressed. *Promotion, or the lack of it, is profoundly significant because, for many, it involves the core of our identity and foundation of our future.*

Promotion, Competition, and Winning

Promotion is intrinsically competitive. It's not an "everybody wins" situation. There's one winner—and the rest are losers. Naturally, everyone wants to be a winner. Everyone wants to be so good that the organization says, "You're so exceptional that we chose you over all the others. We want you to do more important work. You can have more responsibilities. We are giving you more power." Ah, the delicious confirmation of it! "I *am* very good."

In the workshop on plateauing, I ask how many people have significantly more traditional success—more education, status, earnings, or power—than their parents did. Even when the audience is very large, about 95 percent of the people raise their hands.

"How did you get it?" I ask.

"Hard work."

"Who is responsible for your success?"

"*I am!* Nobody gave it to me. I earned it."

Right. In an individualistic and competitive society, we all, as individuals, achieve our success. But then who is responsible for a lack of success? The answer is the same: "I am."

In open, upwardly mobile, and competitive societies, status is earned, it is not a given by birth. When we earn something, we can also lose it. Life is an elevator that goes both up and down. What this means is crucial: we can never take our success for granted.

No matter how confident we are, work is always experienced as a competitive situation in the sense that we cannot escape evaluations of how well we do. Evaluations are not absolute,

they're relative. They always involve an assessment of our performance compared with how someone else did it or is doing it or
might do it. Naturally, unending evaluation and competition create uncertainty about how good we are and increase our need for
reassurance. Promotion is the most real of reassurances and it is,
therefore, the most desired.

A promotion is more than a confirmation of self-esteem; it is
an upbeat, optimistic promise for the future. The promotion creates more possibilities for good things to happen, without end.
Therefore, the reverse—being plateaued—can be woefully depressing.

As part of a career path, promotions tell people where they're
going. It is much easier to strive to accomplish goals that are set
out for you than it is to create the goals in the first place. As long as
they are moving up a promotion ladder, their goals are clear. The
hierarchy of promotions tells them what their objectives are and
whether they're moving toward them. Promotion is thus not only
success, it is also a major way by which people create long-range
life goals.

As long as the hierarchy creates the goal and the motivation to
climb for it, people don't suffer from any existential anxiety about
what to do with their lives. Moving upward becomes the momentum that creates their future. The end of promotions, or the lack of
a ladder, leaves people with the task of creating their own goals
and sense of movement. Not surprisingly, that can result in anxiety
and depression.

At 48, Matthew is two slots down from being the administrator of a very large hospital in San Diego. He was enticed there,
from his previous position as administrator of a small community
hospital in Virginia, with a promise of the top slot in three years
when the administrator retired. That was seven years ago. Alas,
the administrator celebrated his 62nd birthday by announcing
that he was staying on. He's still there. Matthew told me:

> I'm willing to wait a little longer, but I need the
> reassurance from the board that I'm going to get that
> job. I hate to admit it, but I need to know that they're
> confident in me. My need to be promoted isn't a constant
> feeling. Sometimes I think about it a lot and sometimes
> hardly at all. I've done a cracker-jack job and I've
> demonstrated that I can handle the work. I think I'm

better than he is in some ways, and now I need the board
to tell me that they think so too.

In the race to the top, it's not ambition that gets most people,
it's competition. Not everyone admits to being ambitious, but
many people tell me they're competitive. It's easy to get caught up
in the everyday competition of work. And once they're in it,
winning is what counts. Until they're counted out, the pressure of
people moving into their space creates the urge to push them out,
then surge on ahead. After a while, competing is automatic; the
goal of achieving is not nearly as important as being the best. I
think that for those who are very competitive, there is less en-
during pleasure in being the best than there is long-term pain
when they're not. When their internal tape demands, "Be the
best—or else," those people compete all the time. But much of the
time they're unaware of it.

A Case Study of Competition

I've known Michael since he was a teenager in Ann Arbor. He
was a friend of my kids. In those years he was a leader of the more
radical high school clique, and he wore the rebel's uniform: dirty
curly hair falling below his shoulders, long sideburns accentuating
craggy cheekbones, scruffy blue jeans artfully patched with rem-
nants of Mexican peasant weaving, and, long before it became
fashionable, two gold earrings in his left ear.

He went to an experimental high school that attracted two
kinds of kids. One group was made up of real dropouts, early 1970s
teenagers who were into heavy drugs and who hung around the
building because they weren't legally old enough to quit school.
The other group was composed mostly of the very bright offspring
of University of Michigan faculty members. The Harvard-Yale-
Stanford pantheon should have been their natural stomping
ground, but these kids delighted in rejecting the whole scene. That
was Mike's group. Instead of football rallies, Saturday night dates,
and planning how to get into Harvard's pre-med program, these
kids were into free thinking, backpacking, political activism, intimate dialogues, and baking bread with organically grown whole
wheat flour. They relished their nonestablishment behavior, the
required in-behavior for that out-group.

Mike spent four years of high school going to class occasionally but doing no work. Still, he got good grades because he was smart and charming. He didn't know what to do with himself when he graduated so he went to college, in his case New York University. He was, even at 18, tall and unusually sexy looking. He chose N.Y.U. because New York City promised to be a much larger and more exciting playground than Ann Arbor.

In his first year at N.Y.U. he did very well. That is, he got good grades and partied with the best. But he decided to drop out. He said that he needed time to decide what in the world he was doing and that until he did, it was a waste of time and money to stay in school.

He returned to Ann Arbor and decided to be an auto mechanic. He talked his parents into "lending" him $3,000 for a set of professional tools. Since he'd spent most of his adolescence repairing and souping up his own car, he knew everybody in the local garages and landed a job as a mechanic. That's when he moved out of his parents' house and into an apartment that cost $250 a month. He figured that wasn't a whole lot of money because he'd be earning $200 a week.

It took him about a year to learn that being an auto mechanic means, first, you don't always make that $200 a week; second, that $200 a week after taxes isn't very much money, especially when your parents say you can't go home and eat at their house; and third, it's miserably hot in the summer and miserably cold in the winter.

Gradually the glamour of being a mechanic and, more important, a dropout faded. It's tough giving up your antiparent, antiestablishment position when it's been such a source of pride, so at first he would say he'd learned that he needed to make more money. He wasn't ready to confess that he really was part of the upper middle class. So he kept the gold hoops in his ear because those were symbols that he hadn't changed completely.

Since he wouldn't be an auto mechanic for the rest of his life, he went back to school. But he still had no idea of what he wanted to study or what he wanted to do. In school, he found that he was much happier if he made the work very hard, so while he was an undergraduate he talked professors into letting him take graduate seminars. Those classes were made up of serious students, all competing to be the best. That got to him. It became important that his professor and the other students regard him as smart. He still had no idea of what he wanted to do, so testing himself to his limits became the key to getting through school.

Mike couldn't decide on a major so he drifted, taking classes in political science, history, and economics. In his senior year he decided on economics because he had two exciting professors and they agreed to let him do research on his own. It was heady to be regarded as a very promising young man by people whose opinion he respected. But, even as he found himself near graduation, he still had no idea of what he wanted to do in terms of a career.

During the senior year, he felt the pressure of having to make those decisions. Without any real passion, he decided that law appealed to him and so he took the law aptitude exam. He only scored at the 75th percentile. He had no interest in business but he also took the business school aptitude test. He scored in the 99th percentile. Still unclear about what he wanted to do, he applied to both law and business schools. Not surprisingly, he was accepted by some of the best MBA programs but only to medium-prestige law schools. So he decided to go to business school.

His initial response to his fellow MBA students was that he didn't want to have anything to do with them. He said they were smart but they were all nerds. Grade grubbers. He wasn't one of them.

In the first year of graduate school he found he was one of the youngest students; almost all of the others had either another graduate degree, usually in engineering or law, or they had been working for a few years. That made him feel handicapped, and for the first time he decided to shoot for grades.

He had an uncle in corporate financial circles, who gave him an introduction to a vice president of one of the great investment banking houses in New York. Mike applied for their prestigious summer intern program, and was accepted. Simultaneously thrilled and scared, he went to New York the summer following his first year. The internship was serious. Interns were paid at the rate of $40,000 a year, the firm's salary for entry-level MBAs. Here, as at school, the other interns were older, had advanced degrees, and had years of experience Mike didn't have.

During that summer he tried to find out if he would like the work. It was exciting, and that appealed to him. He had to get some idea of whether he was bright enough to succeed. While he couldn't be certain, he thought he might be. The odds of succeeding in that world were very long. But, if you were successful, the financial payoff was unimaginable. So, on the one hand, he became enthusiastic about a career in investment banking.

On the other hand, he looked at what life was like for the

people in the firm. It was obvious that there was no room for people who were only competent. You had to be extraordinary, and that meant working 60 to 70 hours a week. Mike said that price was too high. If you do that, he said, there's no time for play and you better not get married because you'll never have much time for your wife and you'll never see your kids at all. At the end of the three-month internship, he was still ambivalent. He rejected the career because of the personal cost, but at the same time he was seduced by it because the competitive odds were high and the payoff of success even higher.

When he returned to school for the last year of the MBA program, he found the competition among the students even more intense. It became a mini-war for grades and recommendations because it was really a competition for those critically important first jobs. In the beginning he'd called the other students nerds because they were grade grubbers, and now he was doing the same thing. Actually, the competitiveness appealed to Mike because he was a winner.

Increasingly, winning in the out-of-school competition of real-life adulthood became important to him. Mike, the college dropout who wandered back to school because he didn't know what else to do, and who wandered into an MBA program because he did better on that aptitude exam, got serious. He didn't have a calling, but he liked competing. A full semester before graduation, he began strategizing to get an excellent job and he succeeded. He got a job in a New York investment bank, with a starting salary near the top of his class. Then he Went To Work.

I was in New York three months after he started that job and called to invite him to lunch. He suggested that we meet at his office. The receptionist called to tell him I'd arrived, and I sat down to wait. Every time someone came in the inner office, I looked up from my magazine to see if it was Mike. When the fifth person came in, I again looked up and saw a tall young man who wasn't Mike, and went back to reading. Then I heard "Judy! It's me!"

Waiting for him, looking for him, I still hadn't recognized him. With his hair cut short and his sideburns gone, his craggy features were transformed into the rounded face of a Philadelphia Main-liner. Of course the earrings were gone. But nothing could have prepared me for the elegance of his pinstriped three-piece suit and the shine on his tasseled black loafers. I later learned that tasseled loafers are the in-shoes of the finance community.

At lunch, it quickly became obvious that he had silenced any ambivalence about this life. All he talked about was the pressure to learn the ropes. They had given him a lot of responsibility, but school hadn't prepared him for the real business world. So he was working seven days a week. When I asked him how that affected his relationship with his girlfriend, he dismissed my question by saying, "Oh, she understands."

He no longer had any fundamental questions about what he was doing and what the consequences of such hard work could be. He wasn't consumed by ambition as much as he was preoccupied with making it in the competition. He wanted success because he wanted to be a winner. He wanted to be a member of the club.

The bank encourages that driving, ambitious competitiveness by taking it for granted. No performance level is good enough to earn praise. Organizations that assume ambition and competitiveness end up with people who are *very* ambitious and competitive. In those organizations, winning is everything.

What makes people ambitious is their experience of succeeding in the competition. The desire to be a winner brings ambition that is vague in the long term and specific only in the short run. "What am I going to have to do well today? How will I manage this deal? What is it I want to have achieved by the end of this year?"

From the outside, you might look at Mike and say he's ambitious. But he is not ambitious in the sense of striving for some accomplishment, some rung on the ladder. He is not ambitious for anything in particular. He doesn't talk about becoming the next CEO or making vasts amount of money or making some particular sort of contribution.

I think that very few people are ambitious in the sense of having a specific image of what they want to achieve. Most people's sights are only toward the next rung, the next increment of money. Few people start out with specific long-range goals, especially those involving being leaders and having authority and power. In an environment that is competitive, competing becomes automatic and the goal is to be front-runner. Rewards follow being a winner, but mostly what counts is winning for its own sake.

The Cost of Competition

Some try to justify that intense competitiveness by saying that winning is, after all, better than losing. But when winning is *everything*, people get themselves in psychological trouble. If they're not winners, what are they? When promotions end, where are they? For people psyched on winning, there is no middle ground. It's no wonder many people don't know how to cope when they're plateaued. Instead, they deny what's going on.

Denial is a terrible way to cope; reality keeps clanging against your illusions. Denial is no protection. How can you deny that your boss is now younger than you? Wherever there is a hierarchy there is a mental ladder, and people know how far they have progressed relative to their peers. But people try to deny the plateauing reality all the time. In 1981, Professor John Veiga asked over a thousand managers how they would categorize their last job change. He also asked the corporations involved what they would say:[66]

My last job change was a:	The Manager Said	The Corporation Said
Promotion	85%	40%
Lateral transfer	12	51
Demotion	3	9

All people want to be winners, especially those with a long history of being in the front of the pack. Author Gail Sheehy found that Harvard Business School graduates of the class of 1949 were taught, and believed, that unless they were Number One, they were failures. The happiest people in that class are now the presidents of their organizations. The unhappiest are vice presidents. They are so aware of being Number Two that "for the most part, [they] felt cheated by life and let that feeling stain everything else—their marriages, their relationships with their children, even their health. And sadly, most press right on with this unhappy lifestyle unless forced to change . . . so powerful is the illusion . . . within the corporate structure that the brightest and most rational men ignore simple mathematical reality."[44]

That same drive to be Number One characterizes the baby-boomers now in management. *Fortune* found them submerged in work, intensely ambitious, single-mindedly focused on success. The fast-track baby-boomers are "impatient for recognition; they associate putting in time with stagnation. . . . [they are] a brash lot who plan to reap high rewards through a hard-driving, fast charge up the career ladder. . . . To them, being second best is anathema."[71] Predictably, most will not clamber nearly as high as they want to, much less reach the top, so many will be plateauing casualties.

The inescapable fact is that promotions will end for everyone. It is a wretched, widespread, logical, and absolutely unnecessary tragedy that organizations and the people within them do not recognize, respect, and reward all the many plateaued people upon whom everyone depends. Making a value out of always being a winner in the hierarchical sense creates grief and a loss of self-esteem. There are lots of winners and all kinds of ways to win—but not as long as people's own definition and their organization's definition restricts winning to climbing.

When the situation is competitive, as it usually is, when someone else succeeds, we may lose. Our triumph today can always be eclipsed by someone else's triumph tomorrow. As long as we're competing, anxiety never ceases. Our confidence is always contingent on what happens next. We can never take success and achievement for granted. Until we feel successful in our soul—and that is hard to accomplish—the race for success is a zero-sum game in which for every winner, there must be one or more losers.

Plateauing and the Sense of Masculinity

In the same way that we want to create the sense that "I am good," we also want the sense that "I am Man" or "I am Woman." In addition to our general sense of identity and self-esteem, we also strive for success in a gender sense. In the same way that we earn our general identity, we achieve a gender identity.

Men achieve a sense of being man by winning in competition, especially against other males. For middle-class men, the most important turf is work and the second is sex. Success: more money, power, and status—those are things we traditionally associate with men, with masculinity. Those are the things that men translate into a visceral sense of achievement: I command respect from other men. I have responsibilities and power. I am looked up to. Women find me sexy.

Like anything else that you get by winning it in competition, a sense of gender esteem can be lost as well as gained. It's not an attribute you can take for granted, it's not in your hip pocket forever.

For men, the most fundamental gain of promotion, of winning at work, is an increasing certainty that they are men. The most fundamental loss is the sense that they are not.

From the sand piles of childhood to the sandlots of adolescence, the game of life for men is "King of the Hill." Masculinity is traditionally gained by competing successfully. And it has to be earned; it is not a quality we attribute to men just because they are male. Since winning is the most basic source of the sense of masculinity, psychologically traditional men can find it very hard to feel like men when they're not winners any more.

Plateaued men are usually conscious of their fear that they may lose the respect of others. They know the judgmental stereotype about plateaued people. This troubled awareness will be increased if people behave toward them as if they will never become more important and are, therefore, not worth much attention. This attitude is communicated by the fact that others no longer seek their opinion, no longer ask to work with them, no longer try to have lunch with them . . . and they no longer attract sexual curiosity, even bits of flirting, from women in the office.

Power is sexy. Success increases a man's sexual attractiveness. Men who have risen to the top, and those who are climbing, are very attractive. Two professors who examined romantic relationships at work found that in 74 percent of the cases the man was in a higher organizational position than the woman, and concluded that "it seems clear that power and attraction are deeply intertwined in romantic relationships at work."[54]

Because power accrues more power, and because power is erotic to women, then being plateaued, which involves the end of further power, can bring diminished appeal in its wake. The combination of realizations—they're plateaued, they're less sexually attractive than they were, and they're aging—can create fears that they're no longer truly men.

When this idea is presented in a lecture or workshop, the audience tension is awful. The men are very silent. No one looks at anyone else, no one jokes, and no one moves. After a little while, still not speaking, they nod their heads in agreement. Then, sometimes, someone lightens the mood with a macho joke.

More than any other culture, Americans fuse work and personal merit. While American men tend to equate success with masculinity, in fact, most American men actually derive much of their identity from their roles as husband and father, and much of their self-esteem comes from those responsibilities. But they are much more conscious of work as a source of self-esteem because at work they are most aware of ambition, energy, and skill.[6]

Aging adds to the stress of plateauing and increases the probability of despair. The possibilities for promotion narrow most sharply when people are in their forties, when, realistically, they are inexorably middle-aged. Between the ages of 35 and 43, most men feel the tremendous gap between their aspirations and their attainments, between their expectations and the facts of plateauing. They must face the difference between the earlier perception that they were outstanding and the current judgment that they are of average competence.

> I'm 42. I think that's young. The prime of life, as a matter of fact. But right now I seem to be getting some kind of message. Oh, nobody has said anything outright. But, hell, Bob just got promoted to the head of the section and he's only 34. I hate to have a kid over me. I have to admit that he's good. Real good. But I could have done that job.
>
> Is this it? Am I on the shelf? Forty-two and gone as far as I'm going? Why? I'm as good as I ever was. Better. I'm better than I used to be. I've got more experience and I know a lot. And everybody likes me. I could manage this section, I know damn well I could. I'm getting to be the old man here and that's not making me feel any better.

The relationship of status at work to the sense of masculinity and self-esteem is clear even early in a man's life, but until the early thirties, the need for success has a tentative quality. The thirties are the decade in which people have to realize they are inescapably adult; kid time is over. Thus, sometime in their early thirties men become aware that the preparation phases are over and they will be assessed as adults.[37]

In his book *Seasons of A Man's Life*, Daniel Levinson, a Yale professor, calls the years from 36 to 40 the BOOM, the time when a man seeks to Become One's Own Man.[37] This is when men try to assert themselves and achieve independence. They leave the protection of a mentor and the guidance of others. They want affirmation that they are capable and in charge. In these years men want acceptance into the club; they want to be regarded as peers by people they used to see as their superiors. Men want other men, whom they respect, to respect them enough to ask their advice.

This doesn't usually happen earlier because it takes years to gain enough experience and visibility to be seen as outstanding, as an authority.

When that acceptance is given and promotions have taken these men into the upper organizational levels, then they are confirmed by others and can experience themselves as truly men. A qualified success in these years, Levinson says, is not much better than a gross failure. "It is likely to evoke a man's worst fears: that he will never realize his potential, or—the most terrifying thought of all—that the potential was never there."[37]

It is really frightening to think that in the next several decades, large numbers of men will not rise high enough in organizations that they will be able to regard themselves as their own men. Because structural plateauing is now happening earlier, large numbers of men in their thirties will, if they cling to traditional criteria of success and masculinity, never be confident that they are men.

There's one other psychological trouble spot: the notion that providing for the family—or at least being the primary breadwinner—is the man's role. The decades of affluence in which baby-boomers grew up created expectations that they would always live in affluence. The parents of the baby-boomers enjoyed "the good fortune of having their expectations shaped during the worst of times and their achievements realized during the best of times. . . . For their children it is just the reverse. 'It's not downward mobility but upward futility. . . .' "[60] In fact, for many of the boomers, it *is* downward mobility. They will be the first group since 1890 that has not done better than the group before it; they may be the first downwardly mobile generation. "The baby boom generation may never achieve the relative economic success of the generations immediately preceding it or following it."[60]

The boomers are not poor, but they *feel* poor. Things they took for granted when they were growing up—a house, a back yard, a car—are out of their reach. Though their earnings are substantial, they are also illusory because of the long-term effects of inflation and the bracket creep of taxes. Actually, the earning power of many with higher educations has lagged far behind the effects of inflation. The salary of recent liberal arts graduates is running 30 to 35 percent less in real income than for those graduates starting out in 1970.[60]

Those are the economic facts for a generation of people with very high expectations about how they would live. The downward mobility of their actual standard of living has an obvious solution—the dual-career household. In fact, that is what they are doing. In 1990, only five years from now, the prediction is that only 14 percent of the wives of intact marriages will be out of the labor force.[46]

In other words, the men of the baby boom generation *need* the income that their partners can produce if they are to live in any way close to what they expected. That's very different from having your wife work because her salary buys fabulous vacations, gourmet dinners, and antique furniture. At exactly the age when they're striving to achieve the sense that they are men, many will learn that they will never be able to provide for their families the same way that their fathers did. Economic dependence has never been a route by which men have achieved confidence and self-esteem.

The need to generate new values about what a man is, and what success is, will become an imperative for this generation.

Plateauing and the Sense of Femininity

There is a parallel gender issue for women, but the psychological dynamics are the reverse of those for men. Like masculinity, femininity has to be achieved; but while success facilitates the sense of masculinity, it can threaten the sense of femininity.

Women who are ambitious, competitive, and successful will gain self-esteem as the result of winning in the competition at work. But success—promotion—does *not* create the sense that "I am a woman." Since the payoffs of success—increased authority and power—are thought of as masculine, achieving significant success can generate anxiety about whether the achiever is still "feminine."[4] It's much easier for women to feel comfortable about success if, at the same time, they receive assurance that they are women, feminine and lovable *as women*. That's most easily achieved if you're in a relationship in which you love and are loved. But the statistics of loving commitment for successful women are low. For women, unusual success can result in heterosexual loneliness and the anxiety that they are not lovable, that they are not women.

Increasingly, the familiar questions—Is time running out? Did I make the wrong choice? Am I a woman?—beset the unmarried baby boom women in their thirties who set out, in earlier years, to achieve success. Unlike their male peers, the vast majority of whom are married and fathers, the majority of successful women are single. The awareness of age, as the mid-thirties approach, combined with the slowing rate of promotions and the diminished headiness of triumphs, can create an awful fear of permanent loneliness.

When I ask corporate men how many are married, at least 95 percent will raise their hands; the percentage who are fathers is about the same. John Veiga found the same percentages in his study of men who were corporate managers: 97 percent were married and 93 percent had children.[66] The census figures for those never married, divorced, and childless are highest for women who earn $25,000 a year or more and who have five or more years of college. The most successful women are least likely to be married or mothers. The statistical chances of women marrying decline rapidly after the age of 25, and never marrying is particularly likely for women who have a college education and reach 40 without a husband.[61]

Traditionally, women assure their feminity through being loved and loving, usually in marriage, and by having children. It is not a coincidence that for the past five years we have had the highest rate in our history of women aged 35 and older giving birth to their first child. I think that most of these older first-time mothers are women who accepted their shift in priorities and succeeded in gaining an emotional partner.

In 1984, the *Wall Street Journal* and the Gallup organization surveyed 722 female executives who were vice presidents or higher in companies with annual sales of $100 million or more.[57] Some 52 percent were childless. Most were satisfied with their professional and personal lives, but some were a lot happier than others. Married women were more satisfied than those who were unmarried. The unhappiest were the single, mostly young women who felt they had no personal life.

Meet Jennifer, who seems to have it all. She's elegant, tall, slim, and expensively dressed. She's 37 and earns $110,000 a year. That's success! But, speaking softly and a little sadly, she says:

> I've been out of school for eight years. For my MBA I specialized in long-range planning and the timing was just right. When I graduated it was just becoming big and there weren't many experts around. I was hired by one of the largest consulting firms, and right after grad-

uation I was making more money than my father ever earned in his life.

Besides the incredible salary, the thing that really gets you in a company like this is their "up or out" policy. If you're not terrific, you're out. So your pride really gets involved and you end up working 60 to 70 hours a week all the time.

When I was an undergraduate I decided that I was going to go as far as I could, so marriage and children would have to wait. Actually, I really didn't want to get tied down at all. I hardly ever thought about children and the few times I did, I was simply glad I didn't have any.

For about the first six years, I didn't think about much besides work. If for no other reason, I simply didn't have time. I dated some, but it was never anything serious. Most of my social life was with people I met through work, and we were all too busy and preoccupied for anything else. I kept getting promoted and my raises were enormous. I'd say that I was really quite happy until about two years ago when I hit 35.

I'm certain that my work will always be important to me and the challenges are still exciting. I'm up for partnership soon and I'm pretty confident that I'll get it. That part of my life is fine.

But the truth is, it's getting lonely. I used to be glad to come home to an empty house, but now it feels *too* empty. The thing that's really bothering me, though, is I'm getting close to 40. That's getting to be a serious number. . . . I think I'd like to get married and have at least one child. But there's nobody around on the horizon. A lot of the women I know feel the same way, but where are the men?

The chances are good that the unmarried, plateaued, successful women will realize that the cost of their success is not a less fulfilling family life than might have been but, rather, *not having a family at all*. The gut-level fear of these women is that they might not be Women.

Among those in their thirties, there is also a substantial number of angry women. If we take their average age as 35 in 1985, in 1970 they were 20. At that time, there was a small cadre of very influential and angry feminists, especially on university campuses. In those years, radical feminism accepted no compromise with traditional feminine values and lifestyles. The enemy was not limited to the abstraction of a sexist society. Rage was directed specifically at men, so that relating to men meant going to bed with, and becoming a victim of, your adversaries. The women who were caught up in this form of feminism were ideologically committed to living a life that was the reverse of tradition. Since they identified with traditionally male values, they were determined to achieve traditionally male concepts of success.[7]

But now, after more than ten years in the labor force, and with promotions slowing and competition increasing, they have learned what can and cannot be achieved through work. Since they were pioneers, success required enormous effort; when it was achieved, success was exhilarating. But, for most, that heady rush has slowed and the implications are clear when they look ahead and see the executive level, which is overwhelmingly male.

They are now 35, and their age provokes awareness that they are aging. Psychologically, women seem to enter middle age around 33 whereas men acknowledge aging as they near 40. The biological bell tolls earlier and more stridently for women because their personal clock ticks in units of fertility.

These women made a self-aware decision to be "their own person." To them, that seemed to require avoiding any commitment in which they might be expected to be dependent and traditional. With the goal of being liberated, they turned to work for fulfillment. But the pursuit of success is fulfilling only as long as you're winning, only as long as there are more triumphs you can gain.

When age creates the fear that time is running out, and experience reveals that work produces money and status but not love, and promotions are slowing and the job has been mastered, when competition is cruel and being alone is more frequently lonely than free—then these women ask themselves what they have done with their lives and why they made the choices they did.

Those are very tough questions, and there is an awful quality of bitterness in this group. Now approaching middle age, they want love and emotional commitment. Frustrated if they are unable to achieve them, they become angry with the organization where they work because it required so much that there is now nothing in their lives but work. Most poignantly, these women are angry with themselves because they chose what they did. They pursued what men had, but no one told them that, unlike men, they might have to forego love, commitment, marriage, and children—and that someday that might prove to be an unbearable cost.

For women, being plateaued can bring all this crashing down around them. *The issue of what success might have cost them as women may not arise until promotions end.* As long as success is attainable and triumphs are gained, fears of loneliness, anxiety about being women, may lie dormant, alive but silent in the unconscious.

None of the life options for women is easy; each path offers gains and each costs a lot. But women who do it all—pursue demanding careers, are married, and have children—while often terribly harassed, are probably the least vulnerable to becoming plateaued. They have gained social permission to have careers, but they still carry the psychological responsibility of being the main emotional anchor of the family. More specifically, they continue to have primary responsibility for the children. As a result, they are not free to focus single-mindedly on work. They are, however, protected from becoming plateaued for the long term by their emotional commitment to all their major roles.

Promotion Is Complex

While structural plateauing can result in simple disappointment for some, for others—those who have made work their main psychological investment, and who allow success to be their primary source of self-esteem—realizing that they are plateaued can provoke the most basic questions of identity, values, and self-worth. So the issue of promotion is psychologically complicated because it involves people's long-range purposes and their most basic sense of self.

Given the Rule of 99%, too much rides on the fragile barque of promotion. Ambition is an asset when it is followed by success. But ambition that dictates a goal of promotion is ultimately a liability that can cause grievous pain. Too many people who restrict "success" to promotion are frighteningly fragile and vulnerable when promotions cease.

Ambition is an *organizational* liability if structural plateauing creates major frustration, reduced involvement, lessened productivity, and the anger of alienation. An organization may not need the total potential of its plateaued employees, but it cannot afford to alienate them. Yet the logical response to being plateaued is alienation for people with a history of success, in organizations that reward primarily through promotion.[6]

There is nothing quite as convincing as reality. When goals are frustrated by an essentially implacable reality and that frustration goes on for a long time, most people will change their goals if alternative ones are visible and achievable. The next chapter addresses the profound satisfactions that people can attain, throughout their career, when they most respect their own professionalism, their ability to meet new challenges. Then, the most important reward becomes the opportunity to learn and master something new.

The end of old ambitions for promotion can be tough. If all along you've been trying to grab the brass ring on the merry-go-round, and now you realize you can't, that's a big disappointment. But it's not the end of the world. Your task is to change the end of that pursuit into an opportunity to live differently in the next part of your life. Unlike promotion, meeting new challenges, living more fully, experiencing more broadly, and gaining different kinds of success, are major triumphs that never have to end.

5

Content Plateauing:
The End of Challenge

Content plateauing, which happens when work is mastered and there is essentially nothing new to learn, is one of those bad news/ good news stories. The bad news is that people do content plateau; they do the same work for so long that the challenge is gone. The good news is that content plateauing doesn't *have* to happen.

Unlike structural plateauing, which is inescapable, content plateauing need never occur. No one ever knows everything; no one has ever done everything. There are no limits to change and challenge except those created by personal fear or organizational laziness. Content plateauing is preventable and, if it has occurred, is remediable.

At first glance, content plateauing doesn't sound nearly as important as structural plateauing. Actually, I find that the end of the challenge can generate as much stress as the end of the climb.

Since content plateauing results from continuing to do work already mastered, anyone is susceptible to it. Dentists with busy practices can be tired of filling molars; physicians with filled days can be weary of kids with colds; schoolteachers can be bored with the third grade; lawyers can be tired of divorce, pharmacists with putting pills in bottles, accountants with IRS forms . . . anyone can be content plateaued. And the more you know your job, the more likely that is.

It is important to realize that content plateauing is not related to the *amount* of work you do. Your job might be so demanding that you feel harassed. It is possible that you are very successful and content plateaued. If there is nothing new to master and the responsibilities and problems feel *repetitive,* then you are content plateaued.

At 47, Harold looks like he's got it made—a poor boy who made himself a rich man. After ten struggling years as a salesman, when he never made any money, he found a bankrupt hotel he could get control of for $10,000—all the money he had. For the next five years he put in 80-hour weeks, spinning from disaster to crisis, always struggling to stay afloat. Now he has fourteen hotels, all profitable. He has power, status, and money. Today, he looks back and says those were the wonderful years.

About six months ago he realized that he had stopped working *well* some time before. He still spends 70 hours a week at the office, but he really *works* only half the time. He says:

> I feel like an Olympic athlete the day after I got the gold medal. Winning was terrific. It was worth the years of sacrifice. But now it's just details; the big stuff is done. I know how to run a hotel. . . . All my life I've been running as hard as I could, but now there's no point to it and no kicks in it. So what am I going to do?

The magnitude of change that he can imagine creating in his business is too small for him. He needs challenge, and there's simply too little risk there any more. He's done with the mountain he's on; he's reached its summit. He either has to decide that he doesn't want to climb any more, or he has to find another mountain.

Marshall, 43, has been working in a large division of a *Fortune* 100 company for 14 years, ever since he graduated with his PhD. He is seriously dissatisfied with his career. Not only has "success" not resulted in the kind of high he fantasized it would, but worse, he's miserable because he got what he wanted most: the promotion to manager. He finds that being a manger is being a bureaucrat and the work of a bureaucrat is boring. He says:

> The good news is I'm the only one in the whole division with the title of Professional Scientist. Unfortunately, that's also the bad news. I trained as a chemical engineer and my doctorate was in a state-of-the-art

specialty that was pure research at the time. I was hired because they thought the research might have some practical applications over the long run. It took ten years of hard work to get it there, but I did it. For ten years I pushed and I was never sure whether or not it would ever pay off. Every time I got good results I also found another problem I didn't expect.

I thought *that* was frustrating! Now I realize those were the good years because the intellectual challenge never let up and that was profoundly satisfying. Since I pulled it off, I was promoted to Professional Scientist. That was really a kick, but the high didn't last. What this job really involves is pushing paper. I'm drowning in paper! I feel like I never accomplish anything any more.

The need for challenge, the need to burst through the constrictions of tasks and situations already seen and mastered, can affect anyone, even those enjoying the greatest gains from success.

At 48, Rodger was a senior partner in one of the most prestigious consulting firms in the world.[11] At the time, he was supersuccessful. He earned close to $400,000 a year, managed a major segment of the company, served on all the important committees, was regarded as an excellent consultant and an outstanding manager of people, and enjoyed political power. He had only one problem: profound and unremitting boredom. That's not the boredom of "What shall I do today?" It is, rather, the feeling that in the long tunnel of the future there will never be any surprises.

For some years Rodger had been feeling that there were only minor challenges in his job and there wouldn't be any more for him in the company as a whole. He had done everything that you could do as a consultant. He could shoot for the job of president, but that wasn't particularly interesting because it wasn't very different from what he was already doing.

He had been quite troubled for a few years. On the one hand, he thought he *should* be satisfied. After all, not many people get to achieve what he did. But he wasn't satisfied. He entertained vague thoughts about leaving but that felt disloyal. He had been with the company for almost 24 years when one day he received an unsolicited job offer in a totally different business. The next day, he accepted it.

Rodger didn't feel structurally plateaued at all. He had risen high and he wasn't ambitious to get higher. His problem was that while he was busy, he wasn't learning anything. He'd seen all the problems before. He decided to accept the job offer for the simple reason that it was a challenge. Since the work would be in an entirely new area, he might even fail! The new job would be a challenge in which everything was on the line. Engines at maximum rev! Wonderful!

Obviously, Rodger's solution to his life dilemma was helped a lot by years of high earnings and a specific opportunity. Out of the frequently unmanageable universe of possibilities, he didn't have to imagine and choose one for himself. But, more than anything, he had the courage to accept the risk of change.

If you ask people who earn enough to have no significant money worries what they need from their work in order for it to be truly satisfying, this is what they say:

> Impact. Visibility. The work must be important
>   to the organization.
> I have to feel I've been useful.
> Completion. I need to complete a whole project.
> I want to be involved with other people.
> Technical challenge.
> Personal recognition.
> Flexibility and the opportunity to be creative.
> Accountability. My output must be measurable.

Of all possible answers, the most common by far is *challenge.* For professionals, managers, executives, and others in our educated labor force, the absence of challenge makes work dull and dreary. It results in a low-level chronic depression, a daily experience of the blahs.

What Does "Challenge" Really Mean?

Challenge is a 1980s buzz word, so its meaning is not precise. But if you probe, taking the time to ask people what they really mean when they use it, you will find that it means grappling and coping with difficult new issues, whether at work or in their personal lives. Challenge involves change and the growth that results from encountering new situations and problems. Therefore, challenge always involves some risk. More than anything, challenge means learning. It's as simple as that.

In previous years when the world was less affluent, and for

those today who are not economically secure, the sense of challenge is created by scrabbling for survival. But economically comfortable people in a basically affluent society are not satisfied by work just because it enables them to survive. They have different requirements and expectations of life and work. They have psychological criteria for satisfaction, and the most important of them is the feeling that they are always learning and mastering something new. People say, "I want my work to be a source of excitement to me. After all, it's where I spend most of my time. Just earning a living isn't enough."

Mastering something you don't know is engrossing. People usually find the *process* of learning and achieving more fulfilling than the knowledge that they achieve. In that time when we are fully absorbed and engrossed, mastering the task is a high. Motivated to become expert in what we do, the paradox is that we are psychologically most at risk when we are expert because that is when we are most likely to be bored and discontent. We are expert, but the challenge is gone. And, if work is the most important sector in our lives, the danger is that *no* sector feels exciting.

The following was told to me by a manager at a company whose name is a household word, but it could have been said by anyone with a career that is important.

> I sometimes wonder why, when I wake up at three in the morning, it's always because of a work-related idea and not about the roses in my garden. My mental energy is always tied up in work.
>
> Now that I've gotten to where I have, the question is, what am I going to do next? What I need is challenge and success in the future. I mean the need to be accomplish*ing* partially dims my pleasure from having accomplish*ed*. The past is done; it's of no interest now. The thing that really scares me is the idea that there might not be any next challenge.

Learning is an intrinsic reward of enormous importance; for economically comfortable people it is usually more important than extrinsic rewards. Extrinsic rewards—a larger office, a private secretary, a company car, especially more money—are important, but the magnitude of what is gained is usually not large enough to change how we live and thereby justify the enormous commitment we make to our work. If, for example, we make $40,000 a year and receive a 10 percent increase, that additional

$4,000 is taxed at a rate that might result in a net gain of $2,400. If we divide that by 12, the actual total is $200 a month. An intrinsic gain is much more motivating than that.

Basically, human beings like to learn. Therefore, learning is a positive experience and the opportunity to learn is a reward. Moreover, it is an "I" reward, something gained for the inner self. People who have been successful in school and then in the various tasks of work develop a sense of themselves as people who are capable of learning. That becomes an important part of their self-concept, their image of who they are.

Learning thus involves two important motivators: the *experience* of learning, and the *recognition* by others that you are capable of learning. When an organization gives people the opportunity to meet new obligations that require learning, that act says the organization sees them as capable of learning. That reinforces people's sense of their abilities. If, instead, people are relegated to doing the same work for years, the message communicated is that they are perceived as incapable of learning something really new.

Any time there is a significant job change, one in which new tasks have to be mastered, there are three gains. One, the person learns something new; two, the person gets the message that the organization agrees with her own perception of herself as someone able to learn, and three, the person is informed by the reassignment itself that the organization is aware of her. The despair of a plateaued engineer who had been in the same job for 11 years was voiced this way: "Okay. I can accept the idea that everybody can't get to the top of the pyramid, but at least move us around!"

Risk Avoiders, Risk Takers, and Risk Creators

Actually, some people never want challenge. People differ a lot in terms of how much change they can cope with, how much risk feels comfortable. I learned that the hard way.

I once had two receptionists, both responsible for making appointments for students with their academic advisors. They had great big calendar books and every day, all day, they'd write the names of students in the appropriate column for each advisor. They were often busy and sometimes hassled because there were hordes of undergraduates, but it was not an intellectually taxing task.

Word came to me that Betty, one of the receptionists, was

really unhappy. She was single, in her late fifties, earning about $11,000 a year, and she had a master's degree in French. In fact, she had taught French for several years in another university. "Well," I thought, "it's not exactly surprising that she's not satisfied." There was, though, the fact that she had been sitting at that same desk for nine years. Nine years?!

Just about that time, I also heard that one of the staff advisors would be leaving; Betty was an appropriate candidate for the advisor job. The job involved becoming familiar with a lot of regulations, but there wasn't anything intrinsically complicated about them. I was quite certain that Betty would learn them easily. Not only did I have an opening for her, but it had some challenge and paid more money! So, I asked her to come into the office.

"Betty," I said, "I hear you're not too happy with your job. Is that so?"

"Yes," she said, "I really need more money."

"Would you like a somewhat bigger job?"

"Yes, that sounds really nice."

"Betty, we're in luck. Alan is leaving, which means we have a better position for you here. I know you'll be terrific at that job and it pays $3,600 more than you're making now. He's leaving in two weeks and we can hurry the paperwork so you can start right away."

"Dean Bardwick, no one ever took care of me like you. I'm so grateful to you."

Naive fool that I was, I thought that meant she happily accepted the job. Throughout the discussion that followed, she expressed gratitude but mounted objections. When I finally gave up trying to convince her, we said the polite things and she promised to get back to me with a decision, but she never did. She did nothing. She just continued to sit at that receptionist's desk. I assume she's still there.

I was in my Earth-Mother–Manager phase at the time and I felt rejected. It seemed to me that she was too intelligent and educated for her job; in terms of pay, people on welfare made almost as much. She had every reason to take the new job, so why didn't she? In fact, what had kept her at her job for nine years?

The answer to those questions was risk; she was scared to death of it. In the achievement-centered world of the faculty that I lived in, we all accepted risk because our goal was to be on the forefront, the cutting edge of our fields. When your pool is made up of risk takers and creators, you forget that many people experience risk as very scary. They want security more than anything. While their mouths may tell you that they're unhappy and need a change, their feet are stuck in the comforting concrete of predictability.

Changing people's work not only creates opportunities for learning and growth, it also introduces risk. When responsibilities involve material that has not been mastered before, there is some possibility of failure: we can't be *certain* that we will do well. *Risk avoiders are security seekers.* For them, the downside of risk is far greater than the opportunities that change creates.

Most of the people I see in organizations are risk takers. They want a sense of security coupled with a moderate or manageable amount of risk. They know the risks involved in change, but the culture of the organization, the emphasis on success through movement, increases and then sustains their ambitions to move upward. Aware that they could fail at a higher level, they nonetheless accept the risk when the opportunity is offered to them, because their positive ambitions outweigh their negative fears. In the same way, they accept lateral changes because they too are positively associated with movement. Despite any anxieties about success in the next position, they will accept a job change when it is offered.

Risk creators are very different people. Since most are nonconformists, I don't see many of them in large organizations. These are people who intellectually know there are risks but that fact has no emotional reality for them. No matter how successful they might be, when they are plateaued they *create* an enormous change in what they do because they need the exhilaration of having everything on the line. Risk creators do not wait for other people to offer them opportunities; they wrest them.

In a study of very successful men, all risk creators, I found that for them, a failure is just one battle, not the war.[3] They see external barriers to success as obstacles to be beaten or circumvented or turned into opportunities. They can't tolerate being plateaued, and if they are, they don't stay there very long.

Challenge in Phases

There isn't much data available to tell us exactly how long it takes for people to feel content plateaued, but the information we have says that it is difficult to have a sense of learning if your work remains essentially the same for more than three years. Most complex jobs are mastered in that time. If we expand the number of years from three to five in order to account for the different time clocks in people's heads, then that tells us how long it usually takes for the sense of mastery to be replaced by the feeling of boredom if work is static.

Three years agrees with my own experience. The first year I was an administrator I felt like I was tap dancing across the stage of life. I was making decisions when I didn't really know what was going on, trying to look confident, hoping for the best. That was the year I learned. In the second year I knew what was up and I applied what I had learned. I learned some, but not very much. In the third year I harvested—I could run the office out of my hip pocket. In the fourth year I thought I would die of boredom.

People usually go through a three-phase sequence in each new job.[64] The first stage, which typically lasts a few months, is one of socialization. In that time people learn the real parameters of the job: what they need to do and who they have to know. The second phase is one of innovation. With confidence gained in the initial period, employees are psychologically freed from anxiety or uncertainty and they can concentrate on the job itself. This is the phase where achievement is most important and most likely.

It is in this innovation stage, predominantly between the sixth month and the third year, that employees are particularly likely to be satisfied and perform well. In the innovation stage employees experience the increasing task challenge positively, and they are willing to exert greater effort and become more involved in their jobs. That's the period of greatest satisfaction because there's challenge and they know what they have to do to achieve and gain more responsibility and recognition.[31]

After people have been in a job more than three to five years, they slip into the third phase, adaptation. In this stage, even the most complicated jobs may ultimately become routine as people become expert in what they do and too used to doing it. Most employees who have five or more years of experience doing the same work slowly adjust by becoming increasingly indifferent toward any challenge within the task itself. If that dreary state continues and they feel powerless to change the situation, over time they come to prefer and then insist that *nothing* change. The adaptation phase is one of rigidity.

This adaptation is found in all kinds of organizations and all kinds of occupations. Because promotions and even lateral changes slow down when people enter middle age, and middle-aged people can be in the same job for a long time, the resistance to change looks as though it's caused by age. Studies find that people in their twenties and early thirties usually want change because it's seen as a challenge and an opportunity.[56] But by the late thirties, many become resistant to all changes. They don't want new training and new experiences; they want things to remain the same.

All people are judged within a promotion "window"; a time period when they are evaluated for their promotability. Age is a significant determinant of people's relative standing, and age-related evaluations are inevitable. But we are an ageist society; we associate youth with promise and age with the reverse. Our stereotypes about older people ignore wisdom and maturity and emphasize the negative. Older employees are assumed to be less creative, enthusiastic, and efficient than younger employees; and even worse, they're supposed to be rigidly resistant to change and therefore unable to meet new challenges.[58]

When that's what employers expect, that's what they will get. When employees feel like they're on the reject pile and they're afraid because the future yawns as a pit of awful consequences, they'll do whatever they can to hang on to whatever they have. Besides, if ageism dictates that a younger person will be selected over an equally qualified older person so there's no way an older person can win, why try?

When people are both older and plateaued, managers expect them to be inflexible, which really means unable to learn something new. As a result, structurally plateaued older employees are very likely to be content plateaued as well. After all, if you think someone can't learn or won't learn, then you don't ask them to learn.

In fact, most of the time, the relationship between age and a decrement in performance is spurious.[64] Age is not the determinant; the length of time someone has been in his job is. You *can* teach an old dog new tricks.

It's not age that makes people resist change, it's their feelings of failure. By their late thirties, increasing numbers of people are plateaued, stuck on the ladder and in the same job far too long. Grievously hurt in their hopes for success, their confidence ebbing, they don't want any change because they know the negatives of the present and that's as much as they can cope with. Change creates uncertainties and, without confidence, it becomes too frightening. *When people are left in the same job too long, they're receiving a*

*message that perhaps they can't handle anything else. Without the
continuous experience of meeting challenge, it's easy for people to
develop the sense that they can't.*

When people don't have much self-esteem, many try to increase their sense of being secure by making their life predictable.
They don't want any risky surprises. The adaption stage is a
symptom of their depression and fear, but it is an adaption that
creates *more* depression and fear.

People do their best to adjust to their reality. Psychological
rigidity and resistance to change are just the last and most extreme responses when people don't have the opportunity to meet
challenges. If people sense they're not going to get the opportunity
for more challenging work, then a natural psychological defense is
to downplay its importance and not look for it in a sphere where
they can't get it. After a long while, they won't want it; they'll even
fight it, because they're scared of it.

Perspective:
Half Full or Half Empty?

Sometimes people who have been in the same work for a long time
are not content plateaued at all. Challenge is continuously being
created for them because the job keeps changing, responsibilities
are expanding, methodology is continually developing, new problems keep arising, or competition is increasing.

More than objective reality, people's perception of what's
going on, their experience of it, determines whether they're content plateaued. It's a question of perspective. Some people focus on
sameness and others see differences. Those who perceive consisten-
cies will feel content plateaued much sooner than people who
highlight change.

The people whose stories I have described are bored because
they see their work as cycles of endless repetition. "I've seen it all
before and done it all before and the only thing that ever seems to
change are the names." Other people, in the same situation, are
endlessly fascinated.

Irving, now 48, has been a real estate developer since he was
16, when he stepped into the family business. He came to talk to
me because his wife (a social worker) and some of his friends kept
telling him that all he thought about was work and his life was too
narrow. He knew he was supposed to be more rounded, that other

people enjoyed all kinds of activities much more than he did. He could intellectually entertain the thought that he was cheating himself of a wide range of pleasurable experiences, but it had no emotional clout whatsoever. In truth he was a deeply satisfied man.

What he really enjoyed was making deals. New deals can be made endlessly. Sometimes people came to him with deals, sometimes he went out and found them. For him, every new proposal was a head-to-head meeting with someone who wanted to make a profit off him, while he wanted to make a profit off them. Who would win? The money he made was his way of keeping score. Life, for him, was a poker game and every deal was a new hand.

While some people tend to perceive change and challenge continuously, many don't; for them, content plateauing is a major problem.

Stuck in the Same Job!

The worst combination for people who are not risk avoiders is to be both structurally *and* content plateaued. That simply means they're kept in the same job much too long.

Besides boredom or the sense that everything is too repetitive, those people are often resentful and unhappy because they feel that they're taken for granted. And the reason they feel that way is that they are. The great majority of employees are dependable and competent: they are not stars and they create no trouble. When people are competent and no more than that, over time organizations invest less in them. Essentially interchangeable with great numbers of other competent people, they command less and less attention because their potential as individuals is not crucial to the organization.

The few who run the organization and those who are seen as potentially outstanding are nurtured and rewarded. Those who once worked well but whose performance has now fallen off, especially if they interfere with the flow of work, also get attention, either punishment or concerned offers of help. But the majority, those who are no longer rising but remain dependable and competent, who make no trouble but do not shine, are easy to ignore. They are passively punished by neglect. Being ignored is in some way, more eviscerating than being criticized.

At its worst extreme, being ignored makes people feel insignificant. At the deepest psychological level they can feel so insignificant they don't exist. Of all the messages that can be communicated, that is the cruelest.

The message of being insignificant dead wood is communicated by a decline in the informal social exchanges of work, by having little opportunity to give input to decisions, by infrequent performance evaluations, and by being ignored by peers and subordinates as well as superiors. Most of all, the sense that people are taken for granted and forgotten is conveyed by the fact that their responsibilities never change. Those feelings were described this way by a man who had been in the same job for over a decade:

> My ego has taken a beating. I'm making money and that's a better mark of value than the grade level. I'm at the top of my grade in terms of money. But I wonder how others see me. I think I'm better than I'm recognized to be and I'm sure I have lots more to offer than is being used now.
>
> I can understand the fact that there just aren't many promotions lately, especially at my level. But if they don't give me something new and important to do, then I can't really believe them when they tell me I'm doing a good job. The only way I'm going to believe that is when I get a tough new assignment.

Employees can be thought of as stars, solid citizens, or dead wood.[62] Stars are people who are currently doing an outstanding job and who, more important, are identified as the high-potential people who might end up leading the organization. They get the most attention in terms of promotions, transfers, development programs, information on how they're doing, and the like. Solid citizens are plateaued; while they're unlikely to be promoted, they continue to be effective. They are the largest group and they do most of the work. Dead wood are plateaued people who no longer do satisfactory work.

Since the solid citizens, by definition, remain productive, it can be hard to perceive that the organization should be concerned about them, that they might be a silent problem. Solid citizens become a problem when they slip into the dead-wood category. Everyone else receives attention: beginners have training programs, stars have development programs, and dead-wood people have rehabilitation programs. The solid citizens are left to fend for themselves.[62]

When I spoke with Jerry he was an engineering department manager for a major manufacturer. He had been with the company for 22 years and in the same job for 10. He said:

> I miss the vote of confidence that I used to get from a promotion. There's nothing I can do about it and it wouldn't do any good to talk to my boss; he's plateaued too. If he can't help himself, he can't help me.
>
> Right now I feel like I don't get any feedback, not positive or negative. I'm just there, doing my job, kind of a silent citizen. I don't want an atta-boy pat on the back. What I want is a challenge.
>
> After I'd been in this job for five years I realized it would be easy to get complacent and just float along, just survive. That's a disgusting way to live. It erodes your self-confidence. I want to feel like I earn my money.
>
> I don't know why it's this way, but it is. I guess I better look for other mountains to climb.

While it is easy to understand why organizations focus the bulk of their attention on their best and worst performers, over the long haul ignoring their solid citizens is a blueprint for disaster. They are the indispensable people who keep the whole thing running. While any one of them is not uniquely valuable, as a group they are invaluable. Ignoring them, especially leaving them in the same job too long, becomes a message that the organization doesn't particularly need or appreciate or respect them. They must be given the opportunity to make their work challenging; without promotions, that is the only real vote of confidence that will count.

The Good News About Content Plateauing

The importance of the opportunity to learn and meet new challenges should not be underestimated. That is a very powerful value, one that is increasing in our labor force as the number of educated professionals increases. A vice president of a leading electronics firm told me:

It's kind of ridiculous to realize that I've been saying that I'm bored but I was never able to put my finger on exactly what was bothering me until we talked about content plateauing. And you're right when you say you can be content plateaued even though you're very busy. I'm busy, all right, but I'm bored.

This has made me remember something I haven't thought of in years. The most exciting experience I can remember was when I went to the Institute for Managers at U.S.C. Every Monday night 15 of us would get together and talk and argue and analyze case studies. I never knew that learning could be such a stretching exercise. Most of those nights I'd get so high on it that I couldn't sleep.

As structural plateauing increases in frequency, content plateauing increases in importance. Whereas structural plateauing will happen, content plateauing shouldn't. We know that people want challenge. When learning, challenge, is the goal that people want, organizations can provide it. *Because promotions almost always end, and because that is occurring earlier, organizations must emphasize the value of challenge over promotion, because that is a reward they can deliver.*

But that is a very different value than prevails in most organizations. Since changing people's central objective in that way would require an enormous transformation in most organizations' culture and reward system, we have to ask whether there are any organizations that already have those values, and what happens within them. The organizations I know well that operate on the value of challenge for its own sake are the research universities.

We can learn something from the professors in those institutions. There are only three ranks: assistant, associate, and full professor. Promotion from assistant to associate professor must be accomplished within seven years or you are fired. At the level of associate, you normally have tenure and cannot be terminated except under extraordinary circumstances. The pressure to be promoted to associate is therefore fierce, but it cannot last more than seven years. Most faculty who reach full professor do that within ten to fifteen years of getting their doctorate. After that, unless they go into administration, there are no higher ranks. Promotion is important for a limited time only.

What, then, do professors work for? What are their main objectives? They want to create knowledge in the forefront of their field. That's where their egos lie; that's their bottom line.

The faculty members are structurally plateaued early, but most remain involved and productive even after retirement. Unless they lose their enthusiasm and creativity, they need never be content plateaued. Without the external rewards that most people think of—promotions, money, perks—they work full-out long after they get tenure because their work remains terribly hard and immensely satisfying.

As individuals, professors have much greater control over what they do than most people who work in organizations have. Professors in research universities are usually free to choose the subject of their work. They are responsible for the topic, its importance, and the quality of what they produce. They have the freedom and the obligation to choose issues and produce work that their peers will judge to be important.

In general, professors in the research universities, especially after they reach tenure, need never feel powerless in their careers. It is common, for example, to see them change the major thrust of their research about every five years, the same period of time it takes most people to feel content plateaued. Powerlessness is an important reason why plateaued people feel terrible. Organizations must not only create opportunities for people to feel challenged, but they have to involve the people affected in the decisions about what they will do.

All people face the hazard of being content plateaued. The risk rises if they are specialized, older, expert, or self-employed. Most people are bright but not brilliant, or, even if brilliant, not specifically talented. That means they are not particularly "best" at something but, on the other hand, can learn anything in the general domain of their profession. While some expertise is always lost when experienced people move on to something else, in fairly short time they will know that work too. When people have the opportunity to engage in new work, be creative, and make things happen, enormous amounts of psychological energy can be released so that they work well and feel good.

We have increased the problems of people in organizations by emphasizing upward mobility as the way to create change and challenge. Change does not have to be vertical—it can always be created horizontally. At work, there is an obvious way to accomplish that. People have to alter their responsibilities often enough so they are not content plateaued. Their work must change enough that they begin the whole work cycle again: a short socialization period, an innovation stage of three to five years, and, optimistically, no adaptation phase at all.

As long as we associate change with vertical movement, then the tendency is to ignore those who are no longer moving upward. In other words, we create content plateauing *where it need never exist*. Content plateauing is not an integral part of hierarchical organizations in the same way that structural plateauing is. It is an arbitrary outcome that follows from ignoring human needs.

People who are structurally plateaued should not be content plateaued. While structural plateauing is inevitable, content plateauing can always be avoided. Organizations have to separate the plateauing that results from the end of promotions and that which results from keeping people in the same job for too long.

Most people want to be challenged through change—significant enough change that they can recapture the vivid sense that they are alive. That means they want to work fully extended on tasks where they need to learn and have the excitement of mastering manageable amounts of uncertainty.

6

The Sequence
of Disappointment

What do most of us want from our work? Our occupation is a basic grounding of our identity. For those with careers, especially, it is a primary way by which we belong in society. While the truth is that we have as much opportunity to experience satisfaction, fulfillment, and personal growth in our private lives as we do in our work, many of us so value our paid work that we see it as the place with the largest opportunities for the most significant outcomes. Work is, therefore, the sector that we associate with success. At the same time, it brings the possibility of failure. (The same is true of our family, but most people don't think about that until there's a divorce or real trouble with the kids). Downside risk is always proportionate to the size of the upside gain.

It is in our work and not in our families that we have the sense that, as individuals, we did it, we created it or pursued it or achieved it—by ourselves. Even people in what we think of as the most mundane occupations—toll collectors, museum guards, mail carriers—somehow manage to see their work as a contribution, important enough to be done well.

Our work creates our present time and doing it well becomes an anchor for who we are and how we feel about ourselves. For those whose careers are going toward something, our work largely creates our sense of having a future and moving into it. Where else but in our work can we make decisions that change the course of events, even if those events are limited to our department, our organization, or our field? Where but in our work do we have the formal authority and thus the power to make things happen? And if we do work we can regard as important, what we accomplish in our work is, in a sense, our immortality.

Work, then, is where we want to know that we have accomplished, learned, grown, made our mark, made a difference, gained more freedom, made bigger decisions, had a bigger budget, gained more power—were judged by others as winners so we could judge ourselves as winners. In work we have the opportunity to fulfill— or to frustrate—very central ways of how we feel about ourselves.

Workaholics: The Vulnerable Ones

For many, work becomes the only area of real passion. As a result, the rest of life grows paler and increasingly less significant. The people who are most at risk, who are most likely to be miserable when they plateau, are those who define themselves totally in terms of work. In an elemental sense it is who they are. When they're plateaued at work, they feel plateaued in the whole of their lives.

The most vulnerable people are those for whom work is the only emotional commitment. Their self-esteem depends upon success. Work is the only place where "success" is possible. "Success" can be achieved only by promotion. When promotions end, there is no joy in the present or in the perceived future.

The most vulnerable people are workaholics. Being a workaholic is not simply a matter of the amount of time given to work. It's a state of mind, in which work becomes so important that there are no other major commitments, no other sectors where accomplishments seem significant. For workaholics, all the eggs of self-esteem are in the basket of work.

The Most Vulnerable of All

Because I work with managers, executives, and professionals, I see many more men than women and I have a clearer picture of their vulnerabilities. In the discussion that follows I will, therefore, restrict myself to describing men. But if I speculate about successful women, I think that far fewer are workaholics, because women are taught to value and commit to personal relationships far more than men. In other words, I believe the percentage of women whose sole emotional commitment is to work is far lower than we find among successful men.

Merely being in a role doesn't assure that you make a commitment to it—and unless there is commitment, there cannot be any significant gratification. Almost all the men I see in organizations are married and are fathers. While some have a comfortable relationship with their wives and children, many don't. Those who are vulnerable, those who are workaholics, will tell you that they need their families but they no longer feel any passion there.

The vulnerable men see their families as made up of people in separate orbits. They and their wives have grown apart and no longer like to do the same things. They often say they love their wives but have never thought of them as friends. They are much less ambivalent about their children, whom they love more easily but do not feel emotionally close to. They have male friends to do things with and to count on if they got into trouble. But they also say they have no *real* friend with whom they feel emotionally close. Some are aware that they are not even close to their own feelings.

A manager of engineers at a major electronics organization had this to say after I asked him if he was close to his kids:

> I don't think so. Do they come and talk with me about their personal problems? No. I don't feel a close companionship with my kids. I went out of my way to create independent kids, and I guess that's what I got.
>
> I think I've been less than successful in developing aspects of my life other than my work. I don't have any close male friends. Oh, we go out with couples but it's pretty casual.
>
> I look at magazines and periodicals to get as much knowledge as possible, but it's always superficial. I'm trying to understand myself, who I am, and what I really want to do. . . .
>
> I guess I don't know how to understand your question. I don't know how to talk about feelings. I know I should have feelings, but I don't seem to have those experiences that other people describe.

Plateaued men who are in pain tend not to talk or disclose to anyone. While it could help them to talk with others—spouses or lovers or friends or managers—that's hard for them because many men aren't used to revealing how much they hurt. In addition, disclosing how you feel increases your awareness of it. None of the plateaued men that I've talked with had turned to his wife for solace. He can't do it because he's afraid of losing her esteem—and he's afraid he already has with those at work.

Most executives don't have terrible personal lives; it is much more common to find they're just not very good.[9] When commitment, in terms of real psychological involvement, is restricted to work, and work comes before anything else, it's hard to have a feeling of vitality and intimacy in relationships. There's always a chicken-egg relationship: because personal life is not fulfilling, a person withdraws from that sphere and engages in work even more because that is satisfying. And when work ceases to pay off in rewards, then that bitterness spills out into personal life, especially if that sector hadn't been gratifying before.

I find that men who have plateaued and who are in emotionally supportive relationships may still strongly need the success of promotion. The *presence* of emotionally significant relationships does not necessarily diminish the need for further recognition and success.

On the other hand, the *absence* of emotionally important, affirming relationships is usually definitely related to a very intense desire for success because there is a desperate need for more and more confirmation from the organization. When men have no other significant commitments, especially when they're unable to be emotionally close to anyone, they ask their organization to give them *all* the good feelings about themselves that they need. They have nowhere else to get them. The emotional need for promotion is intense because it's their only source of self-esteem.

While a workaholic may look like an organizational asset in the short run, over the long haul the organization will not be able to meet the workaholic's emotional needs. No organization can fulfill all of anyone's needs, especially if promotion is the only thing that counts.

The Sequence of Disappointment: From Rational to Resistant to Resigned

I think I've been sitting at this same desk forever.
All those years of experience and I'm doing Mickey Mouse
   work that anybody could do.
I'm not in the group making decisions any more.

Nobody even asks my advice.
I'm on the shelf. I never thought it would happen to me.
I should be able to make things better.
I don't know what to do.
This is depressing.
But this company owes me. I gave it the best years of my life.
But they're not going to. Somehow I missed my chance. I
    better face it. I'm over the hill and this is as good as it's
    going to get.
What the hell am I going to do?

People who are candidates for promotion want the larger
responsibilities and usually think they could handle them. They
also know that promotions are competitive. While they'll be disappointed the first or second time they're passed over, they're not
likely to be crushed. After all, everyone knows that all the candidates were really good and besides, they're reassured that "something will turn up pretty soon."

Step One: Try Harder

Still, few people want to go through that kind of frustration
again, so as soon as they feel better, most decide to *do* something.
They ask themselves what made them successful in the first place?
They usually say it was hard work—and so they work harder.
    People's first response to being denied a promotion is a *ra-
tional* one. They do more of what made them successful. They
increase the amount they work because it was hard work that got
them where they are. Taking action by working harder is appropriate and constructive behavior. But if they continue to be passed
over, working harder and longer is just the first step.

Plateauing at Home

We can see essentially the same workaholic dynamics and sequence of disappointment among unemployed women who remain
at home if they suffer from feelings of being plateaued because
there's no "promotion" to larger responsibilities and there's nothing new to learn.
    In order to explain why unemployed women have the same
reaction as those in the labor force, I'm going to define "work" as
what we do that we regard as our major responsibility. It is the

sector of our experience in which we feel the most obligation, in which we invest much or most of our self-esteem, and from which we derive much or most of our identity. With this definition it becomes easy to understand why, when work fails to satisfy, being very upset is an appropriate reaction.

In the years when babies are being born and children are in preschool, women can be harassed by the magnitude of their work but still feel good because there's no doubt that their job is really important. It is also emotionally fulfilling. In those years, most women also master other, difficult parts of their work such as entertaining and fine cooking. Like those whose goals are created by the ladder of mobility, the sequence of their goals is created by the age of their children.

But, after a decade or so passes, the children are in school most of the day. It's hard to be a hands-on mother when the kids aren't there. These women respond just like employed people when they are first passed over: they create new goals and expand the domain of their work. This is the period when women typically become more involved with volunteer service, or go back to school, or make an activity such as tennis a serious commitment and work hard at it. As long as these activities are satisfying and create goals they can meet, they can be satisfied.

Step Two: From Rational to Resistant

In the typical sequence when people continue to be passed over, the second phase is one of *resistance;* they resist perceiving what is real. At this point, they work longer in order to keep busy, rather than to work well. They increase the amount of time they give to work but they do not produce more. They say, "I give 120 percent," and in terms of hours this is true. But emotionally depleted, they are neither creative nor productive. In this phase, the reasons for working long have become psychologically complicated.

In the resistance phase, people don't want to perceive the possibility that they are plateaued and they try very hard to pretend that it isn't so. Their denial is helped by other people's discomfort and evasion of their status because no one really wants to give them the news. Awareness that they might be plateaued emerges slowly and inconsistently as they alternate acknowledging and denying it. More than anything, they hope they're wrong and promotion is still possible, but they're continually confronted with signs that they've slipped from outstanding to competent. That's tough on the ego. So while intellectually they may know where they stand, emotionally it's hard to accept or deal with. The resistance period can last for a very long time. I've seen people who have been plateaued for 15 years, still fighting reality.

In the resistance stage, people use *denial,* a simple psychological defense. They deny the probability they're plateaued, they deny they were ever fast-track, they deny their feelings of powerlessness, and they deny being upset.

The following was told to me by a 53-year-old manager of engineers who had been in the same job for 14 years:

> I've not yet admitted defeat. What happens to me, depends primarily on me. Though I'm on a plateau, I'm not willing to accept the finality. There's little I can't get involved in and initiate.
>
> When you realize you're plateaued, it's necessary to get off the plateau. It's an obstacle to overcome. When I didn't get promoted, it was a blow to my ego. But I didn't have an emotional reaction to it. For the most part, I do that in life. Sometimes my wife says, "Stop being so logical."
>
> I'm not plateaued. I have difficulty understanding plateauing. This is the longest I've ever been in a job. . . . If I'm plateaued, it will be personally tough.

The problem with denial is that it doesn't work very well for very long. It's hard not to see that someone else got the promotion you hoped you'd get; it's hard not to see that your boss is younger than you are. But if the issue is exquisitely painful, despite the onslaughts of reality, people can hang on to denial like a drowning person hugs a splinter in the sea. They're desperately trying to see their world as continuing in the same old way and, if you ask, they will tell you they are okay. A 57-year-old vice president of a branch bank said:

> After 20 years with no promotion, and at my age, I know my options are getting smaller. But my ambition never moderated! I guess I recognize the situation, but don't really accept it. I can still get mad and sad, and that coexists with rational control. People who worked

for me are now my bosses. I don't think I'm up for promotion, but maybe I'm wrong. I haven't given up. I don't intend to.

In the resistance phase, issues are never resolved. Instead, people continue to deny being plateaued and maintain a vague hope that there'll be a promotion sometime in a nebulous future. When I ask people who have been promoted within the last three years about their future promotions, they're pretty specific. They usually have a few particular positions in mind and a time frame within which they expect the move to happen. They also talk about how they will make it happen and what they'll do if it doesn't materialize.

In contrast, people who are plateaued, who have been in the same grade or the same job for seven or more years, are vague. They have no specific slot in mind and there is no definite time by which they expect the promotion to happen. They have a general hope rather than a specific expectation because they can then avoid crushing disappointment when they don't get a particular job within a definite time. The vagueness facilitates the denial.

Partly because they don't want to know how bad they feel, people in the resistance phase almost never talk to anyone about the negatives of where they are. If they talk at all, they focus on the positive. They say, "I have more potential than I'm using in this job. I know I have a great deal more to offer and all I want is the opportunity to use it."

In other words, structurally plateaued people will talk about being content plateaued because that can be construed positively. If they are content plateaued, that really means they've mastered the work and are capable of doing something more. They're saying they have more to contribute than is being used. That's a lot different from saying that they feel awful because they're out of the race.

By itself, denial doesn't work terribly well because it's passive, not active, and reality keeps knocking on the door. We usually feel better when we do something about our problems. That's why the most *common* response to the chronic pain of being plateaued is an increase in busyness. That is such a subtle and psychologically efficient symptom that neither the individual nor anyone else may be aware that it is a symptom of major psychological distress.

First, working long hours is appealing as a way to look "good."

Many managers applaud and encourage it. Astute managers often say they don't, but they really do. While they don't tell people to work longer, they do disparage people who work shorter.

A more important reason why people who are in pain work longer and are busier is that they're fighting feelings of powerlessness and insignificance, which are among the core reasons for their despair.

Being passed over a number of times makes people feel their significance is slipping away. So they try to hold on to it. If their job used to take them 45 hours a week but now takes 60, as they bring work home at night and work on the weekends, they can say to themselves, "I know my title hasn't changed, but look at how my responsibilities have grown!" And, as their spouses see how much more they have to work and their friends learn that they don't have time for a game of tennis on Saturday afternoon because they have so much to do, then they too can see how big the job has grown.

The most important psychological gain of the symptoms of working long hours is that when people are very busy, they can avoid thinking about their problems and feeling their bleak emotions. That's why people in this second phase are often as frenetically busy in the rest of their lives as they are at work. They don't know how to cope with psychological pain except by running away from it.

An electronics manager who was working 65 to 70 hours a week, and who had been in the same grade for more than ten years, told me:

> I guess that somewhere in the next three years I better start making something happen for myself. It probably doesn't make any sense for me to wait around for a promotion. I like to work, I really do. Maybe I'm afraid of what will come to mind if I'm not doing anything. I don't sit around like some of my neighbors.
>
> I like to work at home too. At home, all my hobbies have a concrete result. My wife tells me it's an escape. One way to avoid feeling is to keep doing. I'm not sure it wouldn't be good for me to just sit and think more.

Working long is an appealing psychological defense that is particularly dangerous because it's socially approved. This increases people's tendency to do it. The people who are really vulnerable, who are in real psychological trouble when promotions end, are those too dependent on being successful at work. Working longer as a way of coping with feeling bad at work increases the very lifestyle that made them vulnerable in the first place. Worse, this defense encourages the evasion of the real issues, which means they are not solved. Even worse than that, this style of coping is ultimately destructive, because while these people are enlarging the work sector by spending more time at it, they're so tense they don't work well.

Working long but not well means that in addition to the continued frustration of not getting promoted, people who cope in this way also increase their daily experience of being not successful.

The Resistance Phase at Home

Like plateaued people in the labor force, traditional housewives also move into a phase of resistance when their activities do not meet their needs. Many women have become dependent on their children and, as the children grow older and their lives become more separate, the vacuums in their lives make them frantic. They try to deny the extent of their frustration because the consequence of awareness is that they must acknowledge their own responsibility for how they're living, and that is a frightening awareness. Like those in the labor force, they too become workaholics. In this period they clean the house too often, shop for food too often, insist on chauffering the kids despite a car pool—they manage to fill their days.

Since the tasks are repetitive and unnecessary, there is always the danger that the work can feel meaningless and the women, insignificant. If that happens, this solution to feeling plateaued will make them more aware of their passivity, vulnerability, and powerlessness. Like those in the labor force, their resistance period can last a very long time.

Step Three: From Resistant to Resigned

Typically, when people see over a long time that they're not getting promoted but others are, they give up denial and they lose hope. They allow themselves to see a future in which they will not climb. It is then that they enter the *resignation* phase, a time in which they grieve for the ambitions they will never fulfill and for an image of themselves that they cannot maintain. Trying to reconcile themselves to the facts, they say, "I guess that's the way it is. I better stop beating my head against the wall and get used to it."

Basically they're depressed. It's not a deep clinical depression: they don't sit at their desk and weep, they don't sleep too much or too little, they don't eat all the time or stop eating. Rather, they are in a chronic low state in which they walk through work as they walk through life. They have a long-term case of the blues.

This phase is easier for most people to understand and recognize than the resistance phase, and it's easier to perceive the dominant behavior of this period—passivity—as a symptom. While increasing the amount of time given to work is the most common symptom of plateaued people's distress, the passivity that is characteristic of the resigned phase is the most *important* symptom.

Passivity, withdrawal from involvement, is an expression of psychological debilitation, the result of chronic stress. This response is especially important because being passive—not trying to make things happen—adds to people's sense of powerlessness. It's the feeling that there are no options so there are no choices. People feel powerless, so they don't set goals, don't initiate the steps that would make things happen.

Feeling powerless makes people behave in ways that assure that nothing can happen. Thus, the sense of having no control increases powerlessness and despair. Passivity and resignation arise from depression and fear, and add to those feelings. Without initiative and accomplishment, without activity and some purpose, there is no optimism.

Passivity can be seen as a general quality of withdrawal or noninvolvement at work. Or it can take the form of withdrawal from other people, especially because people tend to withdraw from them. At work, plateaued people find it difficult to relate to those with power over them because those are the people who plateaued them. And it's hard to relate to peers and subordinates when you know they know you're plateaued and you're afraid they see you as a loser.

People move toward those with power and, if only for that reason, pay less attention to those who won't get any more. When people are perceived as plateaued, there's a tendency to stop treating them as significant, as people who may gain more power. Over time, gradually, the plateaued people don't get the critical assignments, they don't get asked for advice, they don't get invitations to lunch. *A lack of increasing significance can slowly worsen to a sense of insignificance.* Hurt and angry, people withdraw when others treat them as losers.

An especially significant form of passivity is the absence of anger directed outward, to someone else. Instead, the anger is directed inward, at the self, and is experienced as depression. The people who are in the resignation phase know they feel hurt and disappointed; they acknowledge their frustration. What they are not aware of is the depth of their anger.

They are angry with their organizations because they don't feel utilized enough. They feel angry with their managers because they don't feel recognized enough. And, sadly, they are angry with themselves because of their passivity. They don't initiate, they don't confront, they don't make things happen. They're losing respect for themselves. The dynamic works this way:

> Is this it? As far as I go? Why? I'm as good as I ever was. Better. I'm better than I used to be. I should have been promoted. Damn. If I was as good as I think I am, I could get this organization to do right by me. But I don't seem to be able to.
>
> I'm really angry with this company. And I'm especially mad at my manager. But I better not let that show because then I'd really be in trouble. I deserve more recognition. Why can't I get it?
>
> I hate myself for not making it happen. But I haven't tried much either. I just hope something good will turn up. I hate myself for being so cautious. I wonder why I am.

Passivity in the form of an absence of anger where it is appropriate, or in the form of a lack of initiative or taking charge, can be painful for anyone. It is, however, more difficult for most men because being passive is less acceptable in men. In addition to powerlessness, they may have feelings of impotence because they cannot improve their situation. *Passivity in men can, therefore, reduce feelings of masculinity, which, in combination with the reality of being plateaued, leads to further depression.*

Resignation at Home

In an identical parallel to those who are employed, the resistance phase of housewives can give way to resignation. In this period, a

sense of futility and a mood of depression dominate, often interrupted by episodes of blaming rage. In this period, they can resent
their husbands and their children because they feel taken for
granted, unappreciated, and ignored. Depression, resulting from a
sense of being powerless, is a common emotion among women. It
occurs when they don't see how they can gain control of their lives
without alienating those whom they love and upon whom they
depend.

Unemployed women who are married to successful men are,
today, an especially vulnerable group. In the world of those who
are successful because of what they achieved, only achievement
counts. While women's traditional work is an achievement, it is
not widely regarded that way. It is hard, even for those who do it
very well, to feel equal to those who have succeeded in the
competitive spheres where labor is paid. Without much confidence
or experience in taking risks they're very afraid of failure. Then,
despite knowing they need to change their life, they can't because
the need to be secure and not fail outweighs the desire for change.

Burnout:
Extreme Resignation

Burnout is a syndrome, a cluster of severe psychological symptoms first observed in police officers, social workers, and others in
the helping professions. When, after herculean efforts, they were
unable to make criminals honest and mentally ill people well,
these people became depressed, alienated, and totally depleted.
That is what is now called burnout. Although the syndrome was
first seen in groups characterized primarily by frustrated idealism,
we now know that burnout affects all kinds of people, including
managers and executives.

Those who are susceptible are ambitious, motivated, and
hard-working; they push as hard as they can, constantly testing
their limits.[49] The most crucial cause of burnout is the sense that
you do not control your life and you are powerless to change it. The
burnout syndrome is the extreme cluster of symptoms, seen when
plateaued people feel very bad indeed.

People get burned out when they feel trapped—they cannot
leave, and they cannot succeed. When this kind of frustration must
be endured for a long time, and there's no constructive way to deal
with their resentment, people become exhausted.[38]

Management consultant Harry Levinson has identified the

conditions that are most likely to lead to burnout in managers and executives.[38] There is usually a combination of career failure, disappointment, defeat, and a sense of helplessness. People feel exploited, but there's no way to prove it and no way to change it. Since there are no rewards despite their efforts, they feel that no one knows or cares about them and the sacrifices they're making. The frustrations are inescapable, repetitive, and prolonged. The result is deep sorrow, fear, despair, helplessness, self-pity, and rage—and the emotions cannot be expressed or dealt with.

When people experience large amounts of negative emotions, their energy is drained. Quite literally, they cannot cope with much of anything because they have troubles enough just managing their feelings. That is easy to understand if you make a physical expression of an emotion. It's clearest with a gesture of rage. Try this: clench your hands into fists, raise your arms above your head, and bring them down hard, as though you were pounding your desk. How did that feel? Many people say there is a sense of relief and some report they get an emotional rush.

You will notice that the gesture took a considerable amount of energy. How much energy do you think it takes to feel that way— and then cap it? Clearly, suppressing emotion takes even more energy than expressing it. That's why people who have no productive way to deal with their anger, anxiety, or depression don't cope well at work—or anywhere else.

Most people who are seriously upset because they're plateaued go through the three-step sequence of disappointment because that's the usual response to any really bad news. Of course any one individual may not go through the sequence of rational, resistant, and resigned phases in that order. Some people are never seriously distressed, some go back and forth between phases, and some remain in the resistance phase for an enormously long time. People vary in the routes they use and in the length of time it takes them to get to the last phase of the sequence: being revitalized.

The End of Disappointment: The Revitalized Phase

When people who have been harshly hurt by being plateaued become successful in working through and going past their sense of injury, they are *revitalized*. I use that term because I want to emphasize their energy and enthusiasm. No longer preoccupied by the frustration of their old ambitions, past blocked competitiveness, beyond grudging acceptance, beyond illusions about themselves, they have a new perspective about themselves and what they want from work.

Achieving this new view requires that people look on changing their values and objectives as a positive opportunity. The opportunity can be that of having different goals at work, realistic, reachable goals; or of changing their lifestyles or relationships. With new values, people evolve new objectives to strive for and achieve.

Revitalized people have not given up ambition. Instead, they change what they want to something that feels important to them and that they can get. In order to be satisfied you have to have expectations that are realistic. *At work, you have to give up ambitions for promotion and replace them with ambitions of challenge.*

Until plateaued people face their issues squarely, they exist in anxiety. Anxiety is like a fog—formless and hard to sweep away. Most people do much better when a vague issue is transformed into a specific problem because then they can begin to do something about it.

Psychological problems are never solved through evasion. The anxiety of uncertainty is much worse than the disappointment of frustrated ambition. Reducing uncertainty by having the facts and perceiving reality is critical to people's gaining a sense of control over their lives. When they see what is real, they can take steps to do something; as long as they refuse to "see," they wait and hope that someone or fate or luck will be kind. That creates a greater sense of powerlessness.

Until people who are in despair achieve insight about the present, they create their own continuing pain because they cannot construct a future. They can't move forward in their life because they cannot let go of the triumphs of the past. They don't know where to go or what to do.

People who feel very bad because they are plateaued need to redefine their ambition. In practical terms, people experience a great relief when they give up the goals and illusions about themselves that structural plateauing makes unachievable. When they stop chasing what they can never catch, they are relieved of a large measure of their frustration and sense of futility and powerlessness. Then, they can stop feeling the emotions that depleted them and left them with too little energy. When they give up the old because it no longer serves them well, they are in a much better position to imagine new objectives that *are* attainable.

Career plateauing is a fact of organizations; it is therefore emotionally neutral. Only when it is not accepted as an inevitability does it have powerfully negative impacts on people's lives and on an organization's effectiveness. When people come to terms with it, they can break the downward cycle of disappointment, feel good about themselves, develop new values, and create different options. With a broader concept of success than they had before and with initiatives they create, people can maintain their sense of personal power and gain satisfaction from a different range of challenges.

When people give up goals they can't gain, they also give up the anger and depression and constant use of psychological defense mechanisms that continuously drained them. Then, having much more psychological energy, they are in a position to work well, to achieve, and to relate to others. In the revitalized phase people have achieved a way of looking at themselves and their reality that enables them to experience areas of life vividly, as sources of significant accomplishment and pleasure.

The revitalization phase is, in a sense, easier to achieve for women who have been out of the labor force than it is for men, because the goals are more obvious. Women tend to try something they have not done before. They enter the labor force full or part-time, or they return to school, or they take on larger responsibilities in the volunteer sector. When they do that, they make a commitment toward self-esteem and a greater sense of control over their lives.

It is often a struggle to reach the revitalized phase. Some people achieve it without help, but many do not. They remain in the phases of resistance and resignation. Organizations have a vested interest in helping their experienced employees reach the revitalized stance, because it is only then that those people feel good enough to work really well.

When the organization communicates that it cares about them as individuals and that it respects their goals, and when it creates opportunities for them to face challenge and participate in decisions that affect them, the organization helps employees to reach the revitalized phase.

When people are productive because they're satisfied in their work and their life, they can honestly say, "This is exactly the place where I want to be." Then, even though they're structurally plateaued, they're okay. They're revitalized.

7

Plateauing in Life

Plateauing in life is vastly more serious than either structural or content plateauing, because it involves the sense that there's little fulfillment in *any* area of life. Nothing is exciting any more. Plateauing in life is perhaps not as easy to define as structural and content plateauing, but it is—alas—all too well understood. When people feel plateaued in life, their days become like a movie in black and white. Poignantly, they remember when it was in technicolor. It is like this scenario:

A man pulls into his driveway. It's dark, clearly after six o'clock; the end of the workday. He opens the car door and reaches back for his briefcase. He moves slowly, obviously tired. Midway up the walk to his house he hesitates, takes a deep breath, then continues walking. There is no sense of energy.

His wife hears the car and opens the door. He gives her a perfunctory peck on the cheek. It's a habitual gesture.

She asks, "How was your day?"

"Fine."

He drops his briefcase by the stairs and they walk through the house into the kitchen. They don't say anything. She returns to preparing dinner. He pours himself a drink, picks up the paper, turns on the television set, and settles into a chair. He skims the paper while half-listening to the evening news. After a while she calls upstairs, "Dinner's ready."

The kids come down and everyone sits at the table.

"What did you do in school today?" the father asks.

"Nothing," one kid says.

"Oh, you know," says the other. "The usual."

Conversation finished, they eat.

Soon after dinner, he goes up to his study. At first glance, he seems to be working. But he isn't. He's staring at some papers but sees nothing. Actually, he's thinking. He's saying to himself:

> I'm 47. Middle-aged. And I don't know what to do. My whole life is made up of responsibilities and I'm tired of it. Every morning I get up and go to work and then I come home. When I come home I read the paper, eat supper, do some more work, watch television, and go to bed. Then I get up and I go to work . . . my life is a routine.
>
> My wife is a nice person but we've drifted apart. We just don't like to do the same things any more. My kids are great but they have their own lives. Even the friends we see, we see all the time and that's pretty old too.
>
> I guess my life is pretty much like everybody else's but the truth is, that's not much comfort. I'm feeling old and, damn it, I'm too young to feel old. Work used to be exciting, but it isn't any more. It's hard to face, but I guess I've gone as far as I'm going to. What am I going to do? I hate the thought that this is it, this is the way it's going to be.

His wife comes into the study and looks at him. She hesitates and then asks, "Is anything wrong?"

"No."

She tries once more. "You look like something's bothering you."

He looks up. "No. There's nothing special. I had the usual kind of day."

Is this exaggerated or realistic? For many people, it is all too real. Work, home, relationships—life—are made up of sequences of episodes that are repetitive and gray. Being plateaued in life is more serious than either form of work plateauing because it encompasses the whole of how you feel. While *being* plateaued in life is partially related to what people do, more than anything it is a matter of attitude, of *feeling* plateaued in the whole of your life.

When people feel plateaued in life there are no moments of vivid pleasure or excitement in what they do or the people they do it with. Life is too predictable. For them, it has become dreary. The things they do are repetitions of things they have already done and experiences they have already had. They feel that life is filled with obligations that follow from old commitments, ones they made in the past. They experience each day as a set of responsibilities they are obligated to meet.

These bleak feelings are made worse because the future holds nothing but an unchanged extension of the present. Since their only sense of purpose is to meet old obligations, there are no goals toward which they are striving. With no forward momentum, there is no sense of future; they are moving toward nothing. Without goals, there is nothing that creates a clear sequence into the new territories of tomorrow. Without energy and with resignation, they merely endure.

Being plateaued in life is a psychological state. Some people feel that way because they have so little to do that every day is a long series of hours to be filled somehow. Others feel plateaued despite being very busy because their busyness doesn't fill their essential sense of emptiness. Activities, therefore, do not define who is plateaued in life.

Many people who are plateaued in life, especially workaholic men, are involved in all the major categories of participation— they are working, are married, are fathers, are members of a church, are on community committees, and on and on. The most important aspect of their psychological status is subtle. From the outside, they look committed. But they're not. Although these men appear to be engaged in many spheres, they are not really passionate about anything but the role of work. They plateau in life when they plateau at work because work was their *only* sphere of engagement, excitement, and movement.

Gold Medalists: The Extreme Workaholic

At the extreme end of the roles we play are those who are "going for the gold." They become so involved in achieving one specific goal that the rest of their life falls away to practically nothing. These individuals, whom I call the gold medalists, are the people most likely to feel plateaued in life, because all their mental, physical, and emotional energy is directed to just one event. Without it, there is little that *feels* truly exciting.

Some years ago I visited the home of a man who, at the age of 25, had been a member of a team that scaled Mt. Everest successfully. When I walked into his house, the first thing I saw was a huge photographic mural of the Himalayas. The peaks of the mountains gleamed in sunshine and extended forever into an endless vista. That picture dwarfed everything else in the house in the same way that the triumph of the climb had dwarfed everything he subsequently did. Though he was trained as a physician, after the climb he was never able to settle down and establish a practice. Instead, he worked in emergency rooms a few months every year in order to pay his way back to the mountains. At 25, he had known the pinnacle of achievement; he had a peak experience. Nothing else ever approximated that. He spent the rest of his life trying to find it again, but he never did.

Once you experience the exultant high of triumph, it's very hard to be satisfied with less. The problem is, sometimes it's hard to find again. Then, even though you are objectively successful, you can feel plateaued in life.

This is the special case of the Olympic gold medalists the day after they won their event. After years of discipline and sacrifice, they won. Now that they've got the gold, what will they do?

People who have achieved something very difficult can become addicted to the struggle of accomplishment as well as the taste of triumph. The excitement is in the race to the goal, not in being there. Many of those people are no good at maintaining a system; they're only good at initiating and creating change. Their high is in the creative startup, beating the odds, going for it! Tuned to climbing the mountain to climb, they are existentially lost as long as they're still, even if they're sitting on the high plateau of success. They need a new mountain to climb, and life is flat until they find it.

These people are usually oriented to action. When they're successful and the task is accomplished, they become more and more uncomfortable. The absence of struggle and total commitment makes them anxious. I found that every time very successful men achieved major success and stayed successful so long that the challenge disappeared, they changed their work enough so that they had to begin again.[5] The goal of accomplishment dominated their lives, but they made sure there was never a finish line. They needed the emotional rush associated with high-level risk.

People who are afraid of risk, who need high levels of security and thus of predictability, can lead repetitive lives and not feel plateaued. The increments of change they are comfortable with are small, and they will experience small change as major. They are, therefore, less likely to feel plateaued in life.

The people who are most vulnerable to feeling plateaued in life are those for whom work *is* life. They are in psychological danger when that role no longer provides profound satisfaction in the present and they cannot imagine that it will be better in the future.

For many people, work becomes so major a commitment that it is their dominant role. Over time, work becomes more fulfilling and exciting, more totally involving; as a result, everything else outside work is routinized. Then, when they are plateaued at work and work is routinized, it is *life* that is routinized. Nothing is spontaneous; nothing is satisfying.

Unlike people for whom work is a part of life, the people who are in jeopardy have let work *become* life. They have no sense of self apart from their identity in work. As long as success is achieved in work and work creates meaning and purpose, life is fulfilling. When work no longer has a trajectory toward change and accomplishment, toward some kind of triumph, then life is flat.

The Effect of the Roles We Occupy

We can think of our lives as made up of phases within which we move into and out of commitments, or roles. Roles tells us what to do and tell others what they can expect from us in that role, because there are mutually accepted rules of behavior and obligations that go along with the role. Most of the time we are in a role, and most of the significant choices and changes we make involve taking on or letting go of roles.

Roles are an external structure that we inhabit; when we are in them, they are a powerful influence on what we do and what we experience. That becomes clearer when we imagine specific roles—for example, CEO, mother, husband, student, teacher, physician. Those roles tell us what our responsibilities are and how we should behave. More subtly, the roles prescribe the emotions we are supposed to feel.

When people interact with others primarily in terms of roles, there is usually no emotional intimacy involved, which makes it hard to really understand or empathize with others. The emotional distance between them is likely to grow.

Roles create opportunities to experience but they also exclude other experiences. Plateauing in life is especially likely if life has simplified from multiple roles down to one role, because then our emotional range is narrow. Feeling plateaued in life is essentially the deadening of the capacity to feel.

When you ask people who think in terms of roles to talk about their relationships, they tell you what they *do* with people rather than how they *feel* about them. If they relate to others primarily in terms of the activities they do together, or in terms of the reciprocal obligations of your roles, they define the relationship in terms of what they *do*. That serves to prevent any real intimacy. The result is the awful feeling that they're not emotionally close with anyone—because they're not.

There is considerable pressure on men to appear masculine in all their roles, in all the activities of *doing*, which becomes an image of strength and invulnerability. Men, therefore, may avoid intimacy because they're afraid of being seen as vulnerable. But no one is ever invulnerable. In order to protect themselves from awareness of their vulnerability, men can become insensitive to their own feelings of fear. That tendency is enlarged in the role of work, where feelings are a nuisance that need to be controlled or repressed or denied. People in organizations often exchange pleasantries, operate with formal politeness, avoid situations that could become emotional, and try to smooth over situations where deep emotions have been expressed.[8] Besides, it's more comfortable not to be sensitive to others' emotions that result from decisions you make that affect their lives or that come from your winning and their losing.

As the work role dominates life, the work style can become a general character style. Then men, especially, don't express feelings because emotions feel uncomfortable and they are unskilled in showing them. When emotions make people uncomfortable, they think of relationships in terms of actions, in terms of roles.

A psychological imbalance is created whenever people commit to only one role and the orientation of that role is generalized to the rest of life. The bad fit can be seen when people search for emotional connections in the competitive world of work or where people require emotional distance and a goal orientation in the loving sphere of relationships. Ultimately, those who are expert in only one role cannot understand those who operate in a fundamentally different one.

A middle-aged woman told her husband of 23 years that she wanted a separation. She said that she could no longer live in the mockery of their marriage because she felt taken for granted and used. He is a corporate executive. She said that in all the years of their marriage she had been the perfect corporate wife, the beautiful and gracious possession that he showed off to all the other executives.

She complained that because they moved every few years for his career, she could never have one of her own. Now that the youngest of their children was away at college, she said she was going to work. She is bright, ambitious—and frustrated and angry.

He was very upset by what she said and especially about the idea that she would go to work. Because he earned a lot of money, his first response was to ask if he didn't give her enough. She assured him that he did. But, she said, she needed to earn money of her own. "Then," he blurted out, "what will you need me for?" They both knew that money she earned was a symbol of her desire to become independent.

He was shocked. He thought they had had a wonderful marriage and she told him that it had been awful. While he didn't really understand her, he loved her. He therefore gave her the greatest gift he could in the terms he did understand. He relieved her of responsibilities, of a role. He said she did not have to meet the obligations of a wife: she didn't have to cook, clean, do laundry, or entertain for him. He understood the role of work and thus he freed her from having to work for him so she could pursue her career as hard as she wanted to.

It wasn't enough. She said that what she wanted was for him to be interested in *her.* She said his idea of conversation between them was to talk about the list of things they had to do. She wanted a partner who would be tender, empathic, sensitive, and loving. She wasn't talking about not having to cook.

Long divided from each other because of the different worlds they lived in and expert in their separate roles, in the most basic way neither understood the other. She could not comprehend the magnitude of his gift to her in terms of obligations. He could not understand her demand for emotional responses because they were not part of his personality. What a pity.

Going to Where We're Good

We are all better able to work in our careers when we feel anchored and supported by ties of affection. Very simply, when we are in a relationship that feels good, we can bring more energy to work.

But the reverse is not true. When energy is focused on work, there may be little available for the personal sphere.

The lopsided distribution of psychological energy between work and our personal lives is the basis of the imbalance between the two commitments.[32] We give more energy to work when it has a higher priority and because business makes enormous demands on us. Some studies find that especially successful people are much more involved in their work than they are with their families. It may be that for many people the imbalance is a necessary condition for success.

But the imbalance between our commitments involves more than that. It's easy for work to become the focus of life, because we go to the role in which we are most expert and we move away from roles in which we do not do well. We go to our most expert role in order to *gain* comfort and *avoid* discomfort. With more investment in work, over time, we grow less confident and comfortable in other spheres of involvement and we do them less well. The inevitable result is that we avoid those spheres of activity in which we feel uncomfortable and do poorly.

The two most obviously divergent sectors of life are the personal sphere, which is emotional, and the impersonal labor force, which is non-emotional. Although we may be involved in both, if we really commit to only one, if only one involves us as our work, then increasingly our skills and personality grow to fit one sphere.

The sectors in which we are not really commited do not stay the same. Areas of involvement that do not get attention and receive little energy will deteriorate. The deterioration is easy to understand. Much of the time, any initial imbalance increases because it creates the condition in which success in the commited sphere is very likely and failure in the rest of life is equally likely.

If a husband, for example, consistently puts work before the interests of his wife, she grows resentful as she accurately perceives her relative insignificance. She may respond by demanding more attention or by withdrawing. Either way, he stands accused and knows he's guilty. With a lot of failure in the relationship, even though he's trying to do better, he gets to where he doesn't want to work at the relationship. Meanwhile, the grass of work gets greener and greener because he's successful there.

As we grow more skillful in our work role, we grow increasingly separate from those who do not share the role. Although there isn't a perfect fit between the roles we occupy and our personalities, there is some relationship between them. People who commit to only one major role are not only in danger of becoming plateaued, they are also in danger of becoming so narrow that they cannot respond appropriately within other commitments.

As women and men are increasingly immersed in their traditional work roles, it is easy for them to become psychologically separate. It gets harder and harder to put yourself in the place of the other, to understand and empathize. It just gets harder to connect in any ways at all. The ability to communicate diminishes and, with failure, the desire to communicate goes. After a prolonged period in which you find you do not and cannot connect, the tendency is to give up trying.

When I ask workaholic men if their wives are their lovers, those who are in even modestly satisfying marriages say yes. When I ask if their wives are their friends, their most common answer is, "That's a good question. I never thought of her that way." Which means she's not. Friendship is a relationship between peers. When people are solely invested in occupational success, their peers are restricted to people who succeed in the same way they do. This attitude increases the separateness of the spouses because it verges frighteningly close to contempt.

I had the following conversation with Ken, age 44, a man with a PhD in industrial engineering who has had an outstanding career at a major *Fortune* 100 company. His wife is not employed and the youngest of their three children left for college two years ago.

"How does your wife spend her time?" I asked.

"Oh, she does some good-deed things in the church and she gardens and does some things around the house. She's not very creatively employed."

"You seem to be wondering what she does all day."

"You can certainly say that."

"I also hear a certain lack of respect."

"You can say that too."

"Do the two of you ever talk about it?"

"I'm not sure how to answer that. We talk about what she's doing. She didn't finish college and I encouraged her to go back. She did for a while but then she quit. I know how to manage a lot of things better than I know how to manage my wife or be managed by her."

"It sounds like you've got problems."

"It used to be a problem but now it's simply dissatisfying. I guess I've managed to accept defeat."

The lack of respect is not one-sided. Women who are successful in their traditional work, that of creating relationships and emotional connections, can regard men who are not good in that sphere as failures as human beings.

Relationships often erode slowly, their calm interrupted only occasionally by outbursts of frustration and accusation, the deterioration not marked by many crises. Unremarked, it is ignored. If work is stressful and consuming and the goal is peace at any price, the issue of the quality of the relationship goes underground and "home" is made up of rituals that don't mean much but cost little energy.

In relationships where there are few real exchanges and little communication, people relate to each other largely in terms of the obligations each owes to the other. With no vitality, their exchanges become habitual and are, therefore, incapable of generating any real awareness of each other.

When the imbalance is very great and work has the highest priority, then, win or lose at work, the quality of the relationship is in jeopardy. When the work situation is one of winning and work is a sector of triumph and even transcendence, the reward value of work is increased and it becomes even more important. For men, especially, if the work situation is one of losing, they withdraw from the relationship and don't acknowledge how badly they need emotional support because that highlights their awareness of not being a winner, of not being okay.

Given the combination of an emotionally flat relationship and work that has ceased to be fulfilling, the probability is that one or both spouses are plateaued in life. Many people face their need for change by creating new goals in the work they have been doing or turning to some form of new work. Some people come to a more radical realization, especially if they are plateaued in the whole of life. They decide that they need to change the scope of their commitments. For those who have been most involved in their professional lives, they know that it is in the emotional realms that they are neediest.

The Only Constant Is Change

Being plateaued is usually not awful, it's just not good. Most people don't change in any profound way until they are really unhappy. Even when we know we're in trouble, we don't redress the imbalance in our life, we don't move off the dreary plateau, until there's a crisis. Instead of initiating change and doing what we have to, we try to manage and we deny how bad things really are.

As long as our work is fulfilling, even if it is the major component of our life, we don't feel any emotional imperative to change how we live. We may think that we should, but it is only a nagging idea that we don't do anything about. *The magnitude of change that is required when people feel plateaued in life is so great that it can be very frightening. But despite their fear, people do create the necessary changes because they've come to the point that not changing is an even more frightening prospect.*

Our psychological growth is intertwined with change; neither ever ceases. We mature only when we face our issues and conflicts, and those, too, never end. Change is the only constant if only because we age. Change is the only healthy response to the unalterable bottom line that nothing is ever forever. And change always takes courage.

After living within a lifestyle with specific responsibilities and objectives for about seven to ten years, we are propelled by certain psychological forces, entwined with the facts of our reality, to assess what we are doing with our lives. While it is possible to begin the period of judgment relatively dispassionately, many of us will experience great emotion during the evaluation phase because we always come to the realization that while we attained some of our objectives, others eluded us. An assessment always reveals a disparity between what is real and what we imagined. Even success rarely fulfills our fantasy of what it would be like.

People differ enormously in their willingness to engage in this assessment. It can be very frightening to question the core of how you have spent your life. An evaluation period is made up of judgments, all of which might end with the realization that you need to give up some goals, some of yourself, in order to get something that you haven't had and don't know if you can gain. An assessment can challenge essential values that you previously took for granted.

Men, especially, seem prone to avoiding an evaluation of their lives, because that generates emotion and emotion makes them anxious. For those who are plateaued or nearing retirement, the absence of an aware transition phase is important in itself. You do not initiate the changes that are necessary to get off any kind of plateau without the initial awareness that you are on one. If you are going to do anything, you have to feel that being on the plateau is psychologically destructive and that remaining there will only get worse. *The pain of remaining has to become greater than the fear of changing.*

If there is a crisis, evaluation is inescapable and change is very probable. But when the problem is plateauing, usually there isn't a crisis. Nonetheless, when people are plateaued something is very wrong: the stable, unexamined life has become habit and life's routines have become a rut.

When the last promotion has been gained and there is no higher place to go, when the youngest child has left for college, when economic security is banked, when we've "got the gold," we can most easily realize how our habits of living, which were based on old responsibilities and goals, still persist and unnecessarily govern and limit how we live.

With the awareness that it is we who limit our own options and experiences, we can then move toward new fulfillments. The evaluation period is completed when the imperative need to ask questions and make choices is moderated. Then, with less intense emotions, we are able to accept all or some of our past commitments and values or we begin the transition to new ones. Sometimes we reinvest in our previous commitments but our new awareness helps us to enrich those involvements. Even when we seem unchanged, we are altered to the extent of our self-knowledge.

Some people will not change their lives because they believe that environmental constraints cannot be overcome. Others will not make the changes they need because they are very frightened of the unfamiliar, or they are paralyzed by guilt, or they are passive because of their profound self-doubts.

Some people who are plateaued don't make any changes in their lives because they find predictable routine comforting and psychologically necessary. They want the security of knowing what is going to happen all the time. They like knowing their job so well that they never make mistakes. They want to know that they'll play bridge every Tuesday night and go out to dinner on Saturday with a couple they've known for years. They prefer a life based on the security of repetition and predictability, because that helps them to feel that they have control over their lives. While that life may be comforting, it cannot be exciting. Actually, that life cannot provide any sense of progress because the essence of it is control through repetition.

Most people want some sense of security, which involves some predictability, in how they live. But they also want some spheres in which they meet some risk and experience personal growth. Very few of us can cope with a life in which very little repeats or is predictable. We tie ourselves to some anchors of stability because those give us the courage to engage in risk somewhere in our life. Most of us want a combination of stable commitment and new challenge. Change, then, becomes a matter of altering proportions and intensities in different life phases.

While we never need to be content plateaued or plateaued in life in an absolute sense, in a relative sense we will be. Expert in our fields, with so much invested in our skills and career, few of us are able to leave the area we know so well. Economically and psychologically, we can't afford to. So what we do is compromise. We look for the obtainable excitement of a new wrinkle on an old accomplishment.

Whatever level of success we achieve, our relationship to work, its importance and the amount we commit to it should change in the different phases of our life because what is important changes as we age. For all except the truly exceptional, the centrality of our careers must lessen as plateauing occurs and the opportunities for old kinds of success decline. This means that our development, our evolving maturity as adults, rests on our perceiving new concepts of success at different stages of our lives as our opportunities change. If we are too work-preoccupied to adjust our values and our priorities in accordance with the possibilities that are real, we will end up dissatisfied, frozen in old time, plateaued in place.

Similarly, we've known our spouses and our kids and most of our friends for a long time. There is no breakthrough excitement in old relationships. But instead of giving them up we try to create something within them that give us a sense of newness because, unless we are truly unhappy, it is too harsh, too guilt-inducing, and too frightening to abandon the emotional roots of our belonging.

Being plateaued and, more important, feeling plateaued, are the result of permanent commitments. In the 1970s we created goals of endless fulfillment, of continuous growth and excitement, of life as an endless high. That is simply not attainable. You can reach a high, but once a commitment is made, you can't sustain it. Excitement requires the anxiety of loss; once commitment creates security, excitement gives way to the pleasure of comfort. *Just as structural plateauing requires a revised sense of our personal capaci-*

ties, *plateauing in life requires a revised and realistic sense of life's opportunities.*

All people need meaning and purpose in their life. When people have a sense of purpose they have goals, a sense of personal control, and a conviction that life has meaning. For them, there is a past, a present, and a future. There is no existential vacuum; there is no plateau.

We tend to think of ourselves in terms of roles, so we tend to think of our options, the ways by which we can get off the plateau, in terms of new roles. But roles are not our only options; we are not the sum of our roles. We can also change the kind of people we are.

When we are plateaued we have to perceive it as an evaluation-transition period, as the constructive road that will move us to create the next phase of our lives. Being plateaued is like being on the roundtable in the train yard. As the roundtable moves, the train is turned and redirected onto a new track going toward a new place. In that sense, becoming plateaued is an opportunity to pause, reflect, and change. It is a personal sabbatical, a time for self-examination that becomes our opportunity to grow in ways we never imagined.

8

The Watershed Years
of Middle Age

People can feel plateaued at any age, any life stage. They can feel plateaued any number of times. But for most people, the sense of being plateaued in life occurs when they are, and perceive they are, middle-aged.

Some time during middle age most people have the sobering experience of realizing that they are no longer young. The awareness of aging carries with it the intimation of death. That awareness should, and normally does, generate questions of who they are, what they've done, and what they want to do or become in the rest of their lives. Simply asking these questions creates anxiety. For Americans, age in itself creates stress. And, when structural plateauing has become an inescapable fact, so that the world seems to be validating people's normal self-doubts that they're no longer be winners, that stress rises, sometimes unbearably.

> I may have gray hair, but mentally I'm not middle-aged. I'm not content to just let the world go by. I only think of myself as middle-aged now because I think in terms of the end game, when it will all be over, and how I got there. I didn't do that before. I just have more of a feeling of urgency about promotion. That probably started when I was 40.
>
> Look, I'm 44. I think that's young. The prime of life, as a matter of fact. When I didn't get those last two

promotions I had to wonder if that's it. Maybe I've gone as far as I'm going to. But why? I don't understand it. I'm as good as I ever was. Actually, I think I'm better. I'm better than I used to be. I've got more experience and I know a hell of a lot. And everybody likes me. I could manage this division. I know damn well I could.

Whether the major obligations have been in work or the family or both, for most people, men and women, the opportunities for achievement begin to decline by the time they are in their mid-forties. In middle-age there is a convergence of most of life's great issues.

Some life phases and some commitments lead easily to the next, but some do not. Middle age is a time when most of our commitments are in an end phase. So much is ending, all at the same time, that it can be very difficult to imagine what the next life phase could be. But paradoxically, middle age is both the most stressful and the most optimistic of life phases. Many things end— and that is hard—but more beginnings are possible than at any other time.

Is Midlife a Crisis?

There is nothing mystical about midlife changes. There is no automatic midlife crisis. But there ought to be a midlife evalua- tion, which becomes the bridge to middle-aged transition. In a way, a midlife crisis is the period when there is not yet an answer to the question "What will I do next?"

A midlife crisis is the extreme manifestation of the midlife period of evaluation and transition. Not infrequently it becomes a midcareer crisis, a panic reaction to structural and content pla- teauing. In the years between roughly 35 and 43, when promotions grind down and content is mastered, when the mega-numbers of 40 or 45 or 50 flash neon in the billboard of your mind, when your body is aging but your kids are maturing, people begin to assess what they dreamt and what they have become. Questions arise as they begin the second and possibly shorter half of life: "What is the value of what I have done? What have I gained and what have I lost as a result of the way I've lived?" Those are profound questions, anxious questions.

As long as those issues are paramount but unsettled, as long as people question the value of what they have done and vacillate in uncertainty about what they will do, as long as their very identities are no longer sure, they feel anxious and depressed. Disappointment at work adds to bleak feelings and helps to cause them. But the negative feelings about work also derive from a lack of real satisfaction in the rest of life. For many, concentrating on unhappiness at work is easier because it doesn't involve the awful issues of aging and death and the existential anchor of a long-term marriage.

At midlife, many people have lost one or both of their parents, and that underscores the inescapable reality that life is fragile. That awareness can intensify a need to grab pleasure immediately. The departure of the children, once the central focus of the family, may make vivid the fact that the spouses inhabit the same house but are in no way together. At the same time, the oppressive questions of wondering who you are and what you will do create a sense of profound loneliness. If intimate closeness cannot be found in the long-term relationship, it may well be sought elsewhere. New relationships are new beginnings: sensual, sexual, youthful. Divorce, love affairs, and remarriage can become tantalizing possibilities, a way off life's flat plateau.

Middle-aged people have to face a harsh conflict. They can create a new intimacy but lose the decades of a shared life, or they can remain in the old one but lose the opportunity for a new, uncompromised relationship. Trying to reorient who they are and redefine their marriage relationship are both hard tasks that create further anxieties. But working through the issues, confronting anxiety and fear, is also the way that middle-aged people create their opportunities for profound intimacy.[47]

Successfully grappling with structural plateauing and the issue of aging—yours and your spouse's—results in a release of psychological energy. Then it becomes possible to either reinvest in old commitments because you perceive new opportunities within them, or alter the balance of your commitments because you realize that the old imbalance served to impoverish parts of your life and that you can make new commitments.

Allen, a 53-year-old executive vice president of one of the *Fortune* 500, plateaued himself. For further promotions he would have to move to New York City. But he was based in Tucson, and his wife said that she was absolutely unwilling to move any more because, finally, she had begun a career of her own. Her refusal to relocate was actually a specific manifestation of the fact that the middle-aged-marriage was in deep trouble.

Allen decided that he needed his marriage more than he needed new promotions, and he informed his company that he was staying put. That was an enormous decision: his responsibilities at work were large, but there was no challenge there any more. When he gave up the goal of climbing higher, he created the task of discovering new challenges for himself.

The first challenge was to make the marriage better. That required therapy, because it is very hard to undo 25-year-old habits. In marital therapy, he learned he had a second challenge, that of gaining self-knowledge. He had to become comfortable with his own emotional needs, which he had always thrust into his subterranean mind. Not knowing how he felt had created fundamental loneliness—of himself from himself. When he learned about himself, for the first time, he could genuinely respond to his wife. They gained intimacy at a level they had never had. With those successes, he then faced his third goal. He needs new experiences of mastery, challenges that will require significant learning. He has not yet achieved it, but is in the process of defining it. His midlife crisis is past, for he has left life's plateau.

A midlife crisis is not a failure. It is a "dangerous opportunity."[15] It is not a single event, it is a process—a process of transformation that must take years because the issues involved are so basic. The period of crisis is the result of struggle between the desire for change and the fear of change. If the issues are not evaded but are dealt with, if the sublime task of facing your own mortality is accomplished, the result is profound growth, a reorientation that allows you to give up old griefs and create new dreams.

In their forties, people need to evaluate their life, because that is when both plateauing at work and plateauing at home—plateauing in life—tend to occur. The evaluation is the essential preparation for the rest of life. But an evaluation is hard. It always provokes the realization that there is a discrepancy between what was hoped for and what was accomplished; reality never fulfills all of a fantasy. Even when people are more successful than they had imagined, nothing is ever achieved without giving something up. These are painful realizations, so it is slowly, with resistance, that people give up old assumptions.

When lifestyles and values that have guided people's choices for decades are no longer appropriate, they should be changed. But even though they are eager to make the changes and recreate feelings of certainty, most people experience a long three to five years in which they remain uncertain, which only increases their depression and anxiety. That is difficult enough to cope with in oneself. It is vastly more difficult when these feelings exist in both spouses. Then the emotions are multiplied, and neither can be a source of support for the other. It is, therefore, tempting to flee from the evaluation. Not evaluating yourself and your life when it is appropriate is a sign of massive evasion; it is psychologically unhealthy. The evasion is a sign of excessive fear, and the evasion, in itself, helps to perpetuate the fear. The unexamined is always scarier than that which comes to light.

When people have the courage to make the exploration within themselves, they gain a more valid knowledge of who they are, and that results in a more profound confidence than they ever had. Real confidence comes from knowing and accepting yourself— your strengths and your limitations—in contrast to depending on affirmation from others, from outside.

When people do not fear and flee from an evaluation of themselves and their lives, when they do not evade their most profound issues, they are able to generate energy and purpose. They can make whatever changes they need to in their values, their goals, their lives. Levinson found that the men who transmuted their existential anxiety into a period of growth were able to face their mortality, assess their reality, and examine their internal values.[37] Although they were initially ambitious, they didn't give up ambition entirely when they became plateaued. Instead, they defined the domain of achievement more broadly. Most important, success or the lack of it at work became much less powerful a determinant of how they judged themselves. They moved past old ambitions and created new ones that were achievable. When they worked the issues through, when they faced plateauing at work, they could make the future better because the quality of the whole of life became more important than any one aspect of it.

There's a lot that's hard to accept—your own limitations and those of your spouse, the limitations of reality, your aging. Here's another hard one: you have to accept your own fear. If you flee from it and never really resolve the problems, you spend enormous energy on your psychological defenses, which debilitates you. It is okay to be afraid, but it's not okay to be afraid because you're afraid.

Middle Age:
A Time of Endings

In the youth-venerating American culture, even the term "middle age" has the power to hurt.⁵ Instead of welcoming the surcease from youthful strivings, Americans often resist acknowledging their aging. It is surprisingly easy to maintain the denial. Most of the time you perceive yourself as ageless, the person you have always been. But events—your birthday, a promotion or the lack of one, a divorce, a death, remarriage—make you confront the reality of aging.

Psychologically, middle age has the bisecting quality of a watershed. Youth and preparation are over. Unless you start a new career, a new family, a new lifestyle, unless you deliberately seek new beginnings, the life you are now experiencing is your blueprint for the future.

Middle age is a time to give up youthful naivete. It is a time for considering when you control events and when you are controlled, when you initiate and when you are coerced by the habits of your old decisions. This rational discourse is played against the inexorable foreshortening of your future and the mad feeling that while you are an internally unvarying self—a youthful self—situations, other people, and your body inform you that you are no longer young.

Middle age is a time when people have the frightening realization that the years are passing, unpunctuated by events of great significance. In the earlier years, there were births, diplomas, the move from an apartment to the first big house, the first big promotion. Now, none. Those who feel plateaued in life and who do not undertake new work, a geographic move, a midlife baby, or a new love, can feel themselves gripped with inertia, trying to settle for the compromises that are their reality.

Middle age is a time when you realize that earlier decisions, made lightly, have now become permanent. This *is* your marriage and this *is* your job. Yes, there are some good things, but, you wonder, is this all there's going to be?

Middle age is that peculiar time when you see simultaneously that your future is not endless and at the same time it seems to extend with a frighteningly unvarying script. This is your work; this is your spouse; this is your place; this is your level; this is your life. Perhaps the healthy resolution of the crisis of middle age must start with the internal acceptance that something has ended, that the tasks and responsibilities and opportunities and worries of early adulthood are indeed over. You are shorn of some alternatives, but you are also free from some heavy burdens. You are free to create a more egocentric life, one of beginnings; and in your maturity you are well able to do that. The first task is to work through the grave anxieties about aging and the acceptance of middle age itself. The second task is to create new goals and then to mobilize your resources to create the striving toward them that will become your future.

Differences Between Women and Men

Because of the historic difference in the traditional roles of men and women, and because those have been profoundly affected by feminism, there are gender differences in the content of the middle-age crisis and in the ease with which it can be resolved. Most Americans try to resolve the crisis by creating solutions in work, and secondarily by establishing new sexual and family relationships.

Women, especially college-educated, middle-class women with traditional family-centered lives, tend to become vastly more self-oriented during this period and turn to the marketplace as the way to construct the second half of life.

The initial impetus of the women's movement came from the underuse of educated and able women, bleeding from the shards of their own inability to find happiness in what the world considered "normal" woman's work. Each thought her disappointments were unique; the rest of the world just thought her neurotic. When we look at traditional women who are now middle-aged, we see an entire generation betrayed by a culture that promised happiness if they were good. Although they were very, very good, they weren't happy; their kids grew up, their husbands were at work, and the American Association of University Women turned out to be just a club. The tragedy and the travesty of it—30 or 40 more years of life left to fill and no particular idea of what to do with it.

In order to esteem themselves, people need involvement in tasks they believe are important. It is easiest to romanticize a role that you have had little experience with, and middle-aged women have returned to school and to work not simply for survival but for psychological fulfillment. In this sense I think that middle-aged women, especially those who have not worked seriously, have an easier resolution to the crisis of middle age than do men. Work becomes their major route for internal growth. Unlike men and those women who have always worked and had families, when traditional women confront the issues of middle age, they have available the simple solution of a new role. While they must still resolve anxieties about aging, they may evade philosophic issues of meaning.

Middle-aged women who do not let their fear of failing paralyze them but who construct a future of some significance and some difficulty, who go back to school or back to work or take on big responsibilities in the community, will emerge on the far side of their crisis of middle age more realistic, adaptive, integrated, and complex. Women who make a commitment that reverses or enlarges their previous ones are entering roles that will cause them to grapple full out in tasks that extend into the future.

In the crisis of middle age, women who lived traditional roles have the enormous advantage of being able to say, "This role, which I have been kept out of, this is what I want. These activities, which I have not been able to do, are the things I have been deprived of. These barriers, they are the ones I must get rid of!" Whether true or not, traditional women have the comfort of apparent specificity: they know their general direction and approximately what they have to do to get there, and they know, pretty much, what the problems are. Women can say, "What I have to do is what I have not done."

Most men have not had to choose between the major roles; they worked *and* married and became fathers. In their middle age, men will see that they succeeded or failed, rose or stagnated, found direction or drifted, and they will feel generally responsible for the outcome of their lives. They know they were influenced by factors greater than themselves—by the economy or the corporate structure or the government bureaucracy—but the myth of masculinity lies in individual initiative, and this, combined with the fact that they were not as burdened with constraining family responsibilities as their wives were, forces men to feel far more responsible for their lives than women usually do.

In the middle period of their lives, men, too, are forced to appraise their reality. They are usually not forced *out* of anything, as women are, and so it is more difficult for men to define the problem as nonparticipation, with its obvious solution—participation. Some, of course, will in effect do that. They will say, "I have been too good and now I shall take pleasure in being irresponsible;

I have been a workhorse and now I will be a stud; I wore tweeds and gray flannel and now I will wear gold chains and Georgio Armani." But most men will not find that a real answer, because that is a solution of play and we are still a work-centered and Puritanical people. For most of us, a play solution to the crucial issues of identity cheapens our past and our future.

Thus men, and those women who have participated fully in work as well as in family, will be forced to appraise their goals, their lifestyles, and their values, not from the comfort of specific roles and righteous anger but from the amorphous, anxiety-provoking pressure of creating meaning. It is more comfortable to feel anger, directed toward the outside, than anxiety, which is inside. The most obvious changes are external; they are changes in what you *do*. People who have basically *done* everything, whose lives have included all the major commitments, may have to confront the issues of aging in terms of *who they are*. When their life is plateaued, it's easier to prepare for a new career than it is to develop their "human potential"—whatever that is.

Some, like the risk-creating gold medalists, can always create opportunity and challenge, the possibility for creativity and self-expansion. Every one of the successful men I studied—aged 33 to 49—denied that he was middle-aged.[3] There was no black magic involved; rather, each had achieved a similar resolution to the aging crisis: he created huge, important, risky projects at work. When you do that, you're preoccupied with the effort of suceeding. To cope is to be in a state of *becoming*. It means you have a future and that future is running on and has no end. It means, therefore, not being old.

Full-out striving may, in fact, be experienced not as the negative of not being old, but as the positive of being young. Perhaps peak experiences are those hard, grabbing, sweating, extending efforts that some experience in that fusion of accomplishing and being, in the period when the potential is there as well as the risks. *In the effort rather than the accomplishment, especially in something new and particularly when you can experience it as a contribution, one constructs a future.* The future may simply be the engulfing present, which is the task not yet accomplished.

The people who will emerge more mature and stronger from the crisis of being aware that they are aging, will be those who have been able to create a sense of future. It seems necessary for people to be involved in a commitment that is real. It seems necessary for people to believe that what they achieve is morally good. It seems necessary for people to experience themselves as initiating and controlling change, for then change for its own sake is perceived as exhilarating. It seems necessary for people to experience themselves as coping, as becoming, as they work toward their future, which is also their present. Those who experience the crisis of middle age as a phase of growth are those who are able to make a commitment that fills their present time and extends endlessly forward and thereby creates a future.

Middle Age:
A Time of Beginnings

It is true that middle age is a time of plateaus and endings. It is a time of despair, as you realize that unless you galvanize motivation and energy, yes, this is all there's going to be. Time and opportunity and motivation are shrinking. But it is also true that middle age is the life phase of greatest freedom. Middle age is the time of greatest opportunity because you have accomplished all of society's "have-to's"; you've earned your status as an adult. The obligatory tasks and roles are over. That is real freedom.

For most people, middle age will be the first time they can really select what they will do and decide who they will be. Until then, what most thought of as basic choices were really only minor variations on fundamental decisions that they felt psychologically obligated to make. Most of us have almost no experience in making real choices.

Until our forties, the broad, general sequence of what we do is essentially decided by our environment. Our ambitions, our goals come from outside. After high school we go to college. After college, to work. Within work there are stages of promotions. For the majority there is marriage and then kids. We choose when to marry and whom, but not whether to marry. We choose the kind of work but not whether to work. We modify those great decisions, varying the exact timing, but the essentials are decided by powerful social norms, rules that govern everyone because they declare what is normal. And, once the commitment is made, decades of long sequences of choices are determined by the nature of the commitment itself.

If you are middle class or aspiring working class, graduation from high school is merely the passage to college. In college, there is only one choice—your major. What you do is determined every

semester by the dictates of your professors and by the requirements for graduation. Once you make the commitment to get a
college degree, you do what you have to in school until you have
enough education to graduate.

Depending on the major and the career that flows from it, you
go either to graduate school or to work. Ultimately, everyone goes
to work. In terms of making basic decisions, work operates just
like school. In every career there is a known sequence of requirements and responsibilities that take a long time to learn and earn.
Once you make the commitment to a particular kind of career, the
sequence of what you have to do, and therefore what you want to
do, is clear for a long time. You don't have to choose what you will
do because the future is made up of achieving that long sequence of
objectives.

While it may be realistically difficult to accomplish the sequence of steps at work, psychologically it's easy because you
know where you're going and what you have to do. As long as your
goal is to gain the next rank and you think you might get it, you
keep on going. Since you might not plateau for 15 or 20 years, then
for 15 or 20 years you don't ask yourself what you should do next. If
a question arises, it's usually whether you should move to another
organization where the rise might be faster—not whether to go for
the next rung of promotion. The goal of promotions determines the
sequence of ambitions and thus the sequence of life decisions. *Until
you're plateaued, the choice of what to do is constructed by your
work.* You don't have to face the awesome task of creating a future.

Your goals of achievement, the forms of ambition, are created
by the field and the institution in which you work. That sequence
of "want-to" and "have-to" can easily last 20 years, or until you're
plateaued. If you marry and have children, another set of "want-
to" and "have-to" is created and it, too, can last for 20 years. Much
of what we do in that time is dictated by the ages of our children.
Quite literally, this means that most people have had little practice
in making fundamental choices because choice has essentially
been an illusion. The sequence of life decisions was really made as
soon as the initial commitment was made and the role was en-
tered.

But you can make *real* choices and create *real* beginnings when
those obligatory roles are essentially completed. In an abstract
way, you are free when society has no further roles that you need to
fulfill in order to be regarded as an adult. In a concrete way, you
are free when your daily life no longer centers around children and

you have enough financial security to accept some financial risk. Both the abstract and the concrete freedoms are normal in middle age.

When the "have-to's" are finished, the issue is "want-to's." When there's nothing we *have* to do, we have the freedom of choice. But, inexperienced as we are in making basic choices from an unconfined universe of possibilities, the freedom to choose can become an awful burden. That's one reason why it takes such a long time to create goals and decide on a future based on "want-to's." But we can.

Many people do not make changes in their lives until there is a crisis; then, desperate, they know they can no longer continue to live as they have been. They don't move until the agony of the present eclipses their fear of the future. The danger in that kind of change is that it can be extreme, a radical rather than an evolutionary change, based on a rejection of all commitments from the past.

Proactive change—developing new values and goals in anticipation of needing them—is usually far less convulsive than *reactive* change, which follows the feeling of crisis. Very radical change is often the action of people in despair, who point to some sector of their lives and declare that it is the cause of all their grief. Comfort lies in laying the responsibility for how they feel on something external. Then they can say, "If I can only get rid of this, I'll be happy!"

If you have the sense that your life is plateaued, that should provoke you to make changes. The opportunity to alter your life should be positive, but it will ultimately be a negative experience if you find that you can't change your world or yourself. At its worst, an evaluation phase can be triggered by a crisis that leads to depression or rage or withdrawal. It can make you cling to commitments and values that are no longer appropriate but comfortably familiar. Or, a sense of panic can result in extreme change, one based on a total reversal and discrediting of the past—old spouse, old job, old organization, old lifestyle tossed aside.

When the past is so hard-rejected, it's likely that the real objective of the rejection is not to go forward but to flee from tough issues. Those kinds of changes are not constructive, they're symptomatic. They're a symptom of the stress. Running away is illusory coping, because the baggage on your back, the sack of emotionally unfinished business, never grows lighter.

Maturing is more than a matter of changing. It also involves coping with what you have to do, accepting the compromises and the ambivalence that are an inevitable part of every commitment.

Like every psychologist, I've spent a lot of time with a lot of people discussing problems, focusing on what's hard to do. And I've found that by the time they're middle-aged, most people are mature. They've become wise, knowledgeable, more genuinely courageous, better able to cope with crises, theirs and others. As you experience yourself as successful in some aspects of what you do, in some parts of your life, in some qualities of your character, you can think of those as coping styles you have already mastered. You can bring those skills to any problems that arise.

We always have the choice of perspective—of focusing on what is wrong and missing, or what is right and existing. Think, now, of how full the bottle is, instead of how empty. It's easy to lose sight of what's positive about you or good in your life when you concentrate on what's unsatisfying and needs improvement. Those components of your core self or your life that you do well and are pleased with, can serve as guideposts for future changes that you'll be able to accomplish and that will feel good. In middle age, when you face major problems, know that you already have the major resources to solve them constructively.

When I ask middle-aged people to tell me what they do well, they say:

> I have an ability to make things happen and I enjoy that.
> I'm a good husband.
> I'm a good listener.
> I think I get along with people.
> I communicate.
> I'm very proud of my children and they love me and I love them.
> I'm a good manager.
> I organize things well.
> I have a sense of humor.
> I'm very good at helping people I care about.
> I'm a good friend.
> I find creative ways to solve problems.
> I feel good about my perspective on life.
> I'm honest and ethical.
> I can create an atmosphere of cooperation.
> I bring common sense to a situation.

I demonstrate leadership.
I'm aware of myself for the first time.
I'm a good tactician.
I have good judgment.
I am a responsible person.
I have a very good relationship with my wife.
I am a very good wife and now I'm comfortable in that role.
I have maintained my integrity and have not sold out.

Middle age is value-added.

It's appropriate that your outlook be upbeat! In middle age, your fear of change should be far smaller than your optimism. You have many strengths with which to manage the changes of opportunity that are yours now that the "have-to's" are done.

For six months after I made the decision to resign from the university, people kept congratulating me. I'd say, "For what?" They'd say, "For your courage." I'd say, "What courage?" I know that it was very scary to make such a momentous decision and it took a painfully long time. But once the decision was made, I completely forgot how frightening it had been. Once made, the decision felt inevitable. You have to respect your anxiety and have compassion for yourself. Big decisions *are* hard. That's why they take so long. You have to have patience—with yourself.

Your objective in middle age is not to change your life. Your goal is to change how you experience your life. Sometimes that will require big changes in what you do or who you do it with, and sometimes you can achieve that with essentially small changes. Mostly, you need to come to terms with yourself and alter your attitude about what it is you want and therefore how you perceive what you have.

No one can or should tell you what to do with your life. I am, though, certain that periodically you yourself must evaluate it. And I am confident that when you evaluate alternatives, make choices, and initiate changes, you will increase your sense of confidence, your sense of efficacy, and your sense of control. It is only when you take the initiative that you can know that, within the parameters of what is real, the locus of control in your life is you. That's what you're going for; it's the essence of being able to leave any plateau.

Thus it is in middle age, when the likelihood of being plateaued and feeling plateaued are very high and uncertainty and sadness are very common, that people have, if they work through their fear of change, the greatest possibility of creating a future that fulfills the person they have become. Even more exciting, they are free to create a life in which they can become more complex, more involved, more spontaneous—more youthful, as it were— than they ever were before.

9

What the Executive Level Should Do

Plateauing is a controversial subject in American business, because facing it requires organizations to admit that the big rewards of promotion and money are available for a limited time only. Addressing the issue means that organizations have to say that unless people are very extraordinary, no matter how hard they work, their promotion opportunities are finite. Chances are they will reach their promotion ceiling long before they retire.

Because organizations are afraid that people will lose their motivation to work well if the truth is clear, most avoid the subject. That avoidance creates greater problems, because the value system of promotion penalizes those who are no longer climbing. Promotions reward only those who are continuing to move upward. Organizations don't simply *not reward* those who are plateaued. Instead, they effectively *punish* plateaued people by continuing to promise a reward they don't deliver. Nor do they provide alternative rewards.

Plateaued people are the backbone of every organization. They are owed the opportunity to earn respect and rewards. Without it, no one works well; without it, productivity and creativity must suffer.

The first step in addressing the issue of plateauing must be made at the executive level. It is here that organizational policy and philosophy are set, and they have a tremendous impact on how employees act and react. Executives of an organization are the only ones with the power to take a leadership role in addressing problems created by plateauing. They do that only when the problems are costly to the organization and to the individuals within it.

Every organizational policy solves certain problems and generates others. Organizations that fire seasoned employees tend to avoid the problems created by structural plateauing. But they have different problems, those involving commitment and loyalty. It makes no sense to make a serious commitment to an institution that does not make a commitment to its people. In those organizations people use the company in the same way that it uses them—until something better comes along.

On the other hand, organizations in which structural plateauing is a major issue have a philosophy of *not* firing long-term employees. That policy is simultaneously humane to employees and self-serving to the organization because *those organizations tend to keep people and their accumulated knowledge; they retain the investment they made in people.* When the organization makes this commitment to its people, it enhances the sense of "us," of organizational loyalty, and it expects and receives that extra margin of effort when it needs it.

It's very common to find people who have spent their entire careers in excellent organizations like IBM, GE, Westinghouse, Dun & Bradstreet, Eastman Kodak, Procter & Gamble, and Hewlett-Packard. They aren't looking around for better opportunities in other organizations, they look for opportunities within their own organization, because they've committed to it as it has committed to them.

But the problem for these organizations is that they're likely to have many structurally plateaued people. Since the organization needs continued excellence and productivity from them, it must work to keep their morale high. This means that structural plateauing has to be acknowledged by the organization as a whole, and employees have to be psychologically prepared for the end of promotions. *The organization must value and reward those who are productive but not promotable.* Structurally plateaued people have to be able to win respect.

The Basic Conditions
That Create High Morale

People flourish best and are most effective when they perceive their organization as one of excellence that makes a significant social contribution and a serious commitment to them. They need to know the organization's central goals and especially how their work contributes to achieving them. They want to know that the organization is aware of them and values their contribution. In the best organizations performance criteria are clear, promotion procedures are fair, the mood is informal, leaders are accessible, rewards are frequent, and there is a sense of forward movement and a feeling of "us." The *basic* conditions are always necessary. To some extent, the negative emotions generated by plateauing can be reduced by creating these conditions.

But the executive level must also address the plateauing issue specifically. It needs to:

1. Change the organization's climate through education.
2. Create an equitable personnel policy that ensures due process.
3. Change the structure of the organization.
4. Reduce the importance of promotion and increase the value of challenge.
5. Increase respect for plateaued people who are productive solid citizens.
6. Convey the organization's regard for employees who are individuals.
7. Increase the pressure modestly.

There are never any simple solutions to complex issues, and there is no one answer to the plateauing problem. Every remedy is a change designed to solve an existing problem. If it is successful, it will solve that problem but it will also generate new problems. There are, therefore, never any perfect solutions. There are only improvements.

Change the Climate

I think you can fool some of the people some of the time. But you cannot fool most of the people for any length of time. Evading the truth about the average rate of promotion and the average age of plateauing in order to keep people chasing promotions they won't get, creates frustration and anger. In the long run, not being honest, which is a form of being dishonest, destroys morale.

The first step in changing the organization's culture is education. People should be given the information that will enable them to understand what is going on. Information makes the murky clear. With knowledge, people are able to scale their expectations to reality. Also, an education program is in itself a communication of the organization's concern for its employees.

The most important information concerns the impersonal origin of structural plateauing and its virtual inevitability. Understanding the three kinds of plateauing gives people a perspective that makes it easier for some to seek challenge in employment and others to increase their involvements outside work. The information about plateauing should include the relationship between identity, work, self-esteem, and aging; the appropriate role of work in life and how that changes over time; the interaction between work and personal life; and retirement and second careers.

I've found that lectures, workshops, and personal interviews that emphasize information are very constructive in themselves as well as being the first step in a more elaborate program. Presenting the facts make it possible to emphasize plateauing as an impersonal and normal experience, and that is crucial in removing people's sense of inadequacy. Making the facts visible helps people to accept their status and facilitates the recognition that plateaued people are solid citizens who deserve a lot of respect.

Given the emotional nature of plateauing, it's a good idea to bring in consultants to open the subject because that helps to minimize employees' feelings of being manipulated. The personnel and training divisions of the organization should be given a leadership role in the education program and should work in collaboration with consultants.

Organizations are understandably cautious about recognizing the issue. They're afraid that when the plateauing reality is made public, they will lose people's commitment, ambition and effort. But information about plateauing comes as a relief, not a shock. Problems created by plateauing aren't generated by facing the issue; the problems are created by the fact of being plateaued in an organization that restricts esteem to those who are climbing.

Organizations will not have difficulty finding and developing chiefs even when they're forthright about structural plateauing. Chiefs know they're exceptions to the Rule of 99%. The question is what is best for the Indians who are the majority. In the long term it's better for them and for the organization if the plateauing facts are made clear and, at the same time, they are given the opportunity to achieve different goals and gain other rewards. It's simply not a good idea to keep people wanting what they're not going to get.

An information program is only the first step. Then the organization must *do* something. While people experience relief when plateauing is brought out into the open, that also raises expectations that something constructive will follow. Beginning a program always creates expectations of more change than just talking about it. Some changes, especially those involving significant opportunity and rewards for plateaued people, need to be visible and instituted within six months of the information program.

Plateauing can generate opportunities for personal growth or the diminishment of self-esteem, depending on the values of the environment. If the organization's culture fails to accept the inevitability of structural plateauing, then it cannot help people resolve the emotional issues that often arise. In that case, the organization loses the full involvement, productivity, and creativity of plateaued people. *The organization has to widen its criteria of success so that the majority, who are plateaued, can feel that they are winners.*

Create an Equitable Personnel Policy

It is crucial that the *procedures* of evaluation and promotion provide equity; they must assure fairness. People need the protection of procedures that diminish the importance of internal politics. Fairness is created by impartial procedures that use essentially objective criteria. Equitable procedures must be concerned with performance reports, the composition of the groups who make personnel decisions, and the rights of employees who are being considered. If those procedures exist, they should be visible to everyone. If they don't exist, they must be developed. If there are doubts about fairness, then anxiety, mistrust, and alienation follow.

Solving problems created by plateauing also requires an *integrated* personnel policy. There are at least nine specific issues:

1. The pattern of a normal career
2. Career planning
3. Succession planning
4. Job security
5. Early retirement
6. Demotion

7. Pensions
8. Posting positions
9. Hiring policies

The pattern of a normal career should be determined: how many years in any grade level, and how many levels in a career, is *normal.* That information should be published. It should be made clear that only an exceptional few will exceed the average. At the same time, the system of opportunities and rewards within a normal career must assure that a normal career is a valued goal.

Individual career planning should be available to everyone. Career planning and skill development for the few people of unusually high potential are constant concerns in organizations. But plateaued solid citizens, who may be around for another 20 years, don't get that kind of attention. Plateaued people should be asked what kinds of work they would like to do in the future and they should be helped to gain whatever skills they'll need but don't yet have. They should be given lateral moves and other forms of job changes and the opportunity to participate in training programs. It's a question of respect, of treating their careers as matters of serious importance to the organization. After all, from their point of view, their careers are *extremely* important. The one caution is that career planning for plateaued people must not create further expectations for promotion that are unlikely to be achieved.

Succession planning is a program designed to assure that an organization has qualified people to staff its executive positions. It involves identifying the people with unusual potential and making the appropriate investment in their development. It can be thought of as another way of being honest with employees about their probable level of success. This is a formal procedure that differentiates those who will have a normal career from those who are being groomed to have an unusual one. Since it is an opening for those designated as potential leaders, and it is an early closing of opportunities for those not selected, equity and due process in the procedures are absolutely critical.

Job security structured as an informal equivalent to academic tenure, is more common among organizations than is usually recognized. When organizations have a tenure policy, they also need specific time periods when it's "up or out." A lack of decisiveness about firing people when they're not seen as good enough is destructive to the individual, who is allowed to hang around but who will never be permitted to succeed. When there are no decisive evaluation points, people who are okay but not outstanding are allowed to remain, and they will plateau very early.

Early retirement as a way of easing people out has become more and more common since the last recession, even in organizations with a long history of something equivalent to tenure. As organizational expansion slowed, early retirement became a crucial technique for creating opportunities for younger managers to move upward.

If early retirement is handled well, it can be a desirable option for plateaued people, who can then choose to either retire or begin a second career. It is also an excellent plateauing solution for the organization, because positions can be loosened up where the bottleneck is tightest. But if it is handled poorly, it can be a disaster for the individuals who are forced or lured out *and* for the organization. For the individual it can be a message that after a career of service the organization thinks they are superfluous. And if the organization has not thought through the contributions of individuals, it is in danger of losing its most valuable employees because those people know they can take the retirement incentive package and get another, equally good position elsewhere.

Demotions are also becoming increasingly common; hardly surprisingly, they frequently feel like an awful punishment. In this period when many organizations will not expand, good but not outstanding people are going to have to step down in order for others to move up and gain experience. Demotion, like early retirement and second careers, will have to become normalized, a part of people's expectations of what a career involves. Psychologically, it has to be perceived like structural plateauing: a relatively impersonal and normal experience. The psychological blow should be buffered by a thoughtful and considerate handling of the financial issues.

Demotion can be designed so it is seen as postive and not a punitive action. Some people get to a point where they want less responsibility, and that should be encouraged. People are often demoted because they're not doing well. Most people know when that's the case, and demotion can come as a relief, especially if they're moved to where they are successful. Then people can interpret the downward transfer as a constructive and compassionate effort to place them where they do well. A demotion may require a lot of support from the employee's superiors and, in some cases, professional counseling.

Pensions are a major reason why people remain in organizations although they are plateaued and dissatisfied. If they leave, they lose their pensions. Organizations should consider developing *mobile pension plans* like the one used by universities and colleges. TIAA (Teachers Insurance and Annuity Association) pools the resources of the faculty and the academic institutions. Faculty members can move to any participating school without losing their retirement benefits and without placing a high cost on their new employer.

Posting all job openings can create a problem: having to explain to a lot of unhappy people why they didn't get the job. Nonetheless, on balance, I think it's preferable to post all openings. Plateaued people want to believe the *system* is open and equitable. If they don't know whether they were even considered for an opening, plateaued people often feel very anxious. Since, in general, plateaued people don't feel very confident, I find the best policy is to be forthright. They cope better with disappointment than they do with uncertainty.

Changing hiring policies—selecting more Indians and fewer chiefs—may strike some as a radical recommendation; certainly its wisdom will not be apparent for a long time. Recruitment should be matched to long-range promotion possibilities. In a time of promotion scarcity, an organization might do better if it hired some percentage of people who were willing to work hard but who were unwilling to make work the central focus of their lives.

Of course every organization will look for some chiefs; the issue is percentages. In some organizations I work with, the average grade point average of new-hires is 3.85, often from the most prestigious universities in the country. That academic standing alone tells us that those people are traditionally ambitious. We cannot imagine them happily plateaued in the middle of their career. Organizations should not promise promotions if they cannot deliver them, and if they cannot deliver them, they shouldn't have a policy of hiring only exceptional people for whom promotions are vitally important.

Change the Structure

This is the most fundamental of the changes and probably the most difficult to implement. When promotions are scarce, executives have a choice: they can either prolong the appearance of promotions by increasing the number of titles and grade levels, or they can *reduce the importance of promotions by reducing the number of hierarchical levels.* When there are fewer levels, less upward movement is possible. People's attention is then directed laterally, toward possibilities for challenge, rather than vertically.

I have a lot of respect for people's basic common sense. So, I think nothing is gained, and much can be lost, with a pseudopromotion, a gain in title but not in responsibilities. The puffery of a title or a fractional grade increase is a short-lived high when promotions are crucial to people; a new title is not a promotion, and an ostensible change in grade doesn't result in more responsibility or power. A janitor is still a janitor even when the title is Custodial Engineer.

Anger and frustration about not being able to climb higher are proportionate to the organization's emphasis on climbing. That, in turn, depends upon having a large number of very visible rungs and tying all rewards to climbing. If there are fewer rungs and people can get major rewards without climbing, climbing isn't so important. In organizations with crowded ladders, having fatter rungs and fewer of them will be less frustrating in the long haul.

In a structural sense, the end of promotions is caused by the shape of the organization. Organizations should examine their structures to see if modifications are desirable. Different parts of an organization can be designed to be more vertical or horizontal, depending on which is more appropriate. The more horizontal the organization, the greater the distribution of decision-making power and therefore the greater the number of positions involving significant responsibilities.

Increasing the number of autonomous or semiautonomous groups is sometimes an appropriate way to increase opportunities for participation in different and increasing levels of responsibility. It can also be the structural basis that creates a greater emphasis on group values, group success, and organizational involvement. That's desirable if an increased involvement in groups reduces the stressful emphasis on individual competition and upward mobility.

Some organizations have found it constructive to limit the size of units so that whenever a division, for example, gets beyond a certain size, it is divided and another unit is constructed. Besides creating more management positions, keeping units small increases employees' sense of belonging and of personal power, because management is much more visible and accessible. Hewlett-Packard is well known for keeping its operating units to a maximum size of between 1,000 and 1,500 people and, not coincidentally, is famous for the "walking around" style of management.

Increase the Value of Challenge

Executives must provide the leadership for a new focus that makes job change, for its own sake, a normal and valued outcome. Organizations need a policy of lateral transfers for plateaued people at least every five years. Management has to be willing to move experienced but unpromotable people because they respect their need to keep learning. Even when promotion is not in the offing, people want more autonomy and expanding opportunities to achieve. At its simplest, people want their time at work to be absorbing; when they're content plateaued, those hours are boring.

When employees move from overlearned responsibilities to new ones, some challenge is created. At the same time, a job change is a communication to the employees that the organization is aware of them and is confident they can cope with the new work. A major cause for depression among plateaued employees is the sense that nothing is going to change in their work future. Change for its own sake, even if it is not very large or permanent, can be a very positive experience.

It's obvious that the opportunities for job change are much greater if there are transfers between units. Therefore, the executive level needs to create coordinated efforts for lateral transfers between units. That tends not to happen, for two reasons. If the number of employees is very large and they are dispersed in a dozen different operating units, the task of identifying and then matching people to opportunity is huge and requires centralized control. Equally important, managers are unwilling to give up their stars and assume that other managers are willing to give up only their dogs. Since the majority are neither stars nor dogs, but fall in that broad category of competent citizens, managers have to be encouraged or required to release some of their dependable people and take in others. That is more likely to happen if some significant rewards are dependent upon managers' initiatives in this area.

If organizations really want to increase the importance of challenge, good performance should be rewarded with the opportunity to do new work. In other words, if people perform well they get the chance to do something else that appeals to them. *Meeting challenge and mastering it should be significantly rewarded.*

Some of the traditional rewards, ranging from increased autonomy and salary to publicity and symbolic recognition, have to be uncoupled from promotion. It's especially important that a fund of money be available to reward people who succeed in new positions but are not promoted. Instead of across-the-board annual merit increases, raises should be used thoughtfully so that those who learn and produce the most get the most money. Meeting challenge will become a very significant goal if it is significantly rewarded.

Challenge and a sense of career movement for specialists and technical people are frequently provided by creating a system of "dual ladders," one for management and the other for professionals who do not wish to move into management. While I think it's a good idea to have a dual-ladder system, the emphasis for professional people should not be on upward movement but on *the opportunity to do increasingly independent and challenging work.*

That's because the two ladders are not equal. People on the technical ladder don't have the same status as people on the managerial ladder, because final decisions are made by managers and not technicians. This difference in power reduces the motivational reward value of climbing the technical rungs and lessens the importance of technical mastery. If it is appropriate, technical people should be given more decision-making authority. But that will always be limited relative to those who have the perspective of management. Therefore professional people, especially, should be rewarded with challenge, autonomy, and the opportunity to retrain.

Very few organizations offer enough education or retraining for technical people to remain current or for people to switch to different work. Major efforts in training and retraining, in collaboration with systematic efforts to provide job challenge, are critical in meeting the issue of content plateauing and in raising people's confidence and self-esteem.

ITT Educational Services recently commissioned a study of retraining practices and surveyed 322 senior human resources directors from *Fortune* 1500 companies. It reports that about 12,000,000 American employees are now obsolete.[63] Among those most in danger are engineers and technical people, because their "shelf life" is shrinking.[12] As the pace of technological change keeps accelerating, technical professionals are reaching obsolescence at increasingly younger ages.

Three-fourths of the personnel directors reported that their employees wanted retraining. But the survey found that only 36 percent of those large corporations retrained their experienced engineers or technical people or middle managers. Instead, the majority either hired new employees to replace the obsolete ones, put them in jobs that required no new skills, or just got rid of them. That's a lot of wasted experience and a lot of human tragedy. It's especially sad since the data clearly show that when older employees are continuously updated, they are as productive as younger workers, if not more.[12]

There are two sides to this coin. Employees don't do enough to educate themselves, and employers don't make it easy enough or valuable enough for people to invest in training. People will engage in serious education only if it is a mainstream activity in the organization. The organizational climate should be one in which people are *expected* to educate themselves.

I'd like to make a case for giving employees sabbaticals. Sabbaticals are wonderful for renewing the soul, but in this context I believe they're also optimal for achieving retraining. Taking one course a semester is better than not taking a course. But I think that being able to return to school full time for a semester is educationally more effective than five courses taken over five terms. A full immersion allows an integration of material and thus the possibility of far more creativity than just dipping a toe in the water.

Increase Respect

The executives have to be clear about the organization's goals so they can articulate how people's work contributes to reaching them. This requires a specificity about goals that is sometimes hard to achieve but is nevertheless vital. People need to know the organization's progress toward its central mission and understand how their part contributes. This has to be articulated again and again, because when people don't have that sense of the big picture, it's easy to see only details and feel insignificant. *The organization must continuously inform plateaued people in very specific ways that it needs and values their contribution.*

In order for plateaued people to maintain a sense of self-esteem, they have to be judged; their performance has to be evaluated seriously and frequently. That's a significant way of informing them that they and what they do are considered important. Compensation, feedback, and performance appraisals have to create a sense that their work is important enough that it needs to be evaluated.

Nothing creates more self-respect than being included in the process of making decisions. *Plateaued people should be included in decision-making groups, especially those which have the responsibility for doing in-depth studies or creating long-range plans.* The recommendation that organizations foster a culture in which employees at all levels are involved in decision-making is usually justified in terms of "soft" measures. Professor Daniel Denison looked for "hard" measures and found that companies with a culture of involved participation actually gained a return on their financial investment that was nearly twice that of traditional, authoritarian companies.[16]

Convey Regard for the Individual

The presence or the absence of small courtesies can go a long way toward making people feel good or making them feel abused.

I was once working in a *Fortune* 500 company, where the manager of engineering restructured his division in a way that changed almost everyone's job. He planned to announce the changes, which affected about 600 people, at a large meeting in which there would be a wall-size diagram indicating everyone's new position. His plan was efficient but very dumb. He'd have hundreds of people scurrying around, squinting at the wall, trying to find their new place.

That plan was also an insult because it communicated the sense that people were not important as individuals. The need to be respected as an individual is always present. But it is especially important for plateaued people, who are vulnerable to feeling forgotten and insignificant.

In this case it would have been optimal if the head of engineering had discussed the changes with everyone individually, but the numbers made that impossible. The next best thing was a letter. We decided that he would hire temporary clerical staff and write a personal letter to all 600 people, which they'd receive before the meeting, saying, in effect, "This is your new job, this is who you will be reporting to, and I hope you enjoy your new work."

It doesn't take much to make people feel respected as individuals; it just takes thinking about it. In a sense, all the recommendations in this chapter are intended to increase respect for plateaued people. But here is a cluster of additional, though unrelated, specific suggestions.

Organizations should recognize their contribution toward encouraging people to become workaholics. The organization has to challenge its own belief system that the more time and energy it can squeeze out of people, the better. Encouraging employees not to be workaholics is self-serving to the institution because in the long run workaholics become a liability. It has to educate its employees about the long-term debilitation that results from a life dominated by work.

Respect for individuals includes the recognition that *people may have different amounts or kinds of ambition at different times in their lives.* Organizations should respect the desire of mature employees to change the implicit contract. A climate that makes it acceptable for people to plateau themselves structurally, to refuse geographic transfers and promotions because they don't want to work harder, is good for the organization and for the individual. The end of the work-dominated phase of life has to be perceived as a normal development in middle-aged people.

Creative alternatives are needed so senior people can contribute their wisdom while they move aside and others learn the most effective use of power. Organizations will benefit if they *encourage people to use their knowledge in new ways at work, or increase their achievements outside of work.* Visibly successful managers and executives can be given formal responsibility for being mentors to promising younger people. Some of these people could become in-house consultants, or serve as liaison to the community or local government. Plateaued experienced people should be considered a vital organizational resource, and roles should be designed for them so that they contribute what they uniquely know.

Organizations can encourage people to *find a sense of achieve-*

ment and opportunities to contribute in external organizations. IBM, for example, has allowed employees to take social service leaves, on full pay, since 1971. More than 600 IBM employees have been loaned to community organizations and about 500 more have taught at educational institutions. Teaching inside or outside the organization is a role that recognizes expertise and provides a sense of generative contribution. That same sense of contribution can be achieved when mature people take on serious leadership roles in their community.

It's very hard for most people to stop working. I therefore think it would be a good idea for organizations to *create a transitional retirement period* of some two to three years, in which people work half time. During that period, employees could receive a proportionate fraction of their salary and all the benefits. Polaroid, for example, is experimenting with a program in which older workers gradually reduce their hours.[1] Job-sharing, special assignments, and consultant roles are other techniques to accomplish the psychological preparation for normal or early retirement.

I've found that most depressed plateaued people have no real physical activity. That is a significant omission both in terms of their physical condition and in the management of stress. Organizations should *consider having athletic facilities within their plant or encourage the use of external ones.* Depression is a common stress reaction, and moderate exercise, in coordination with training in stress reduction or relaxation techniques, is very effective in reducing depression and increasing the feeling of well-being.[43]

Plateaued people are often desperate to talk with someone. Organizations need to *create a climate in which it is okay to seek help with personal problems.* In general, therapy should not be done in-house because the personal circumstances and emotional status of the employees must remain their own private concern. As a group, plateaued men are eager for information and understanding but have little insight about themselves. They gain major relief when they have the opportunity to talk about their lives with someone who really listens. I don't want to call that psychotherapy. It's more of a conversation, a period of reflection, in which they have a chance to learn about themselves. I'm so impressed with the value of this simple intervention that I recommend that organizations provide this kind of interview session for everyone, with an external counselor, perhaps once a year.

Organizations must encourage plateaued, mature people to create

new initiatives at work and offer opportunities for different kinds of
contributions, so that individuals rely on themselves rather than on
the organization to better their lives.

Increase the Pressure Modestly

While it's currently fashionable to emphasize the effectiveness
of positive reinforcement, I've always found that it's a good idea to
have a little cayenne pepper sprinkled on the honey that attracts
all those flies. In other words, *large* amounts of positive experiences
and *small* amounts of negative pressure help people to remain
aware of how sweet the sweet is. It's a matter of proportion—
without any negative, it's hard to remain appreciative of what you
have.

What kinds of negative pressure? *"Raise the bar,"* for one thing.
This means that productivity is expected to increase. The trick
here is that the higher goals must be specific and almost certainly
achievable. Increasing performance requirement creates negative
pressures on underproductive employees, but has a decidedly
positive effect on those who are successful. Raising the bar provides an edge of excitement and involvement, which increases
motivation and has a good chance of increasing achievements and
the sense of success.

Some rewards, especially pay and bonuses, must be contingent
on performance. Some percentage of people's annual raises must be
for individual merit and not part of an across-the-board increase
or a cost of living adjustment. In too many organizations there's
too little pay differentiation between medium and high performers. In short, there needs to be a direct connection between
work output and the magnitude of rewards.

Even in organizations with policies of job tenure, it's necessary to *discharge* a very small number of people who've been given
every realistic chance to improve their performance, but don't.
People should know that it is possible to fail and be fired. *A visible,*
in-house, outplacement program is a continuous reminder that jobs
can be lost. Outplacement facilities were designed to help people
find new jobs and maintain a sense of self-respect. Nonetheless, the
existence of the outplacement program is a moderate stressor.

Demotion should not be used in the same way, as a punishment. If it is used as a form of penalty, the natural response is
anger, with the likely outcome that the person will work badly.
Demoted people remain in the organization, so demotion must be

handled in such a way that demoted employees do not become continuous centers of discontent.

Some Final Words

I hope it's become clear that plateauing is a problem that executives can successfully address. The worse decision is to ignore it. Then the problem feeds upon itself, as frustration and alienation reduce involvement and productivity, and also self-esteem and self-respect. The poor, the powerless, and the unproductive somehow manage to get poorer, more powerless, and less productive. Successful intervention by organizations is both socially responsible and economically appropriate; it can make employees more satisfied and productive within the opportunities available to them.

When organizations can no longer give people rewards they used to give, then they have to give different rewards, and the new rewards have to be regarded as valuable. And the people who are no longer in a position to gain the old rewards must be given the opportunity to achieve the new ones. More than anything, structurally plateaued people have to be able to earn respect. When they respect themselves, they are in the best position to create a new perspective, one in which they realize that they have an opportunity to continue contributing and to gain other kinds of satisfactions from an expanded life.

10

What the Manager Can Do

Managers have an enormous amount of power over people's lives and how they feel about themselves. From either a business or a humanitarian point of view, managers should know that they can do a great deal to help employees cope with plateauing. And in the process, they will also help themselves, because plateauing is an issue for them, too.

To accomplish that, managers must use various forms of reassurance and communicate the fact that employees are valued, because plateaued people often feel unrecognized and taken for granted. People need to know that the organization, in the body of their manager, is aware of them, esteems them, and values their contribution.

In order of their importance, these are the ten most important things that you as a manager should do:

1. Make the facts visible.
2. Come to terms with it yourself.
3. Counsel people.
4. Eliminate content plateauing.
5. Let people know you know they're there.
6. Create new rewards.
7. Encourage initiative.
8. Discourage a workaholic life.
9. Give honest appraisals.
10. Manage by "walking around."

Make the Facts Visible

Plateauing is a painful subject. Whenever it's discussed, there's usually a lot of tension at first, but then there's usually relief. As long as the subject is avoided, it's hard to clarify what's happening so it's hard for people to think through what they should do. As long as the subject remains in the closet, it's taboo, and that makes it hard for people to talk about it and lighten their emotional burden. Managers need to know the facts and present them to their subordinates. They need to create an atmosphere in which subordinates can discuss the subject, because that helps people to face the issues and form more realistic expectations about promotion opportunities.

The facts about plateauing, especially those that explain the origins of structural plateauing, are immensely reassuring. Since the general rate of structural plateauing is the result of impersonal factors, and since everyone will eventually plateau, the facts make plateauing a normal phase in all careers. That information is crucial, because it challenges the belief that plateaued people are examples of the Peter Principle.

People need to understand why they may feel very bad. The manager can explain the relationship between work and personal identity and self-esteem. There needs to be a discussion about the relationship between an employee's work life and personal life and the psychological impoverishment that frequently results when there is only one significant commitment in life. People need to know that it's normal for their involvement in work to change as they age and that changes will occur throughout the adult years of their lives.

People also need to know that major changes in values and lifestyles are profoundly unsettling and that it's appropriate to feel anxious during the transition. That knowledge reassures people; it makes what they are experiencing predictable.

The most important gain of learning about plateauing is that the phenomenon can be seen as a *normal* experience that repeats in different sectors of people's lives, and everyone has to deal with it. In my experience, people gain a great deal of relief when they are given the facts and the concepts that they need to think about what they *can* gain from work. When they understand the three kinds of plateauing, they have the conceptual tools they need to think about how they might alter how their lives.

Come to Terms with It Yourself

Plateauing is an issue that is close to the emotional bone, and managers are not exempt from its tensions. People can be very upset when they're plateaued, because it brings into question how good they really are and how wisely they've spent their lives. In order to help employees, managers have to have faced these issues and resolved them for themselves. You cannot handle people who are emotionally upset if the same issue is also a major stressor for you. You must not bring *your* emotions to *their* issues. Managers who have not come to terms with plateauing will not be able to deal effectively with others for whom it is a problem.

In addition, as a manager you are both a representative of the organization and an individual whose judgment directly affects that person's life. As a result, you can be the object of more rage than is appropriate. If plateauing is not an emotion-provoking issue for you, you're in a much better position to maintain objectivity or psychological distance even if the employee is very emotional.

Managers who are themselves plateaued can be especially vulnerable if subordinates see them as powerless, as people who haven't been able to do anything for themselves. Sometimes employees are resentful because they see plateaued managers as blockers, people who stand in the way of their promotion. Those kinds of feelings in subordinates can increase the manager's bleak feelings and make the subject harder to deal with. Those attitudes and that amount of emotion have to be dealt with through an honest discussion of plateauing.

The sequence of changes that plateaued managers need to go through are:

1. *Know* the facts about the causes of plateauing and the emotional responses that can result. Your goal is to be able to understand the three forms it can take and talk about them.
2. *Feel* your own emotions as you think and talk about plateauing. Try to distinguish the most important feelings for you. Your goal is to really know how you feel.
3. *Act* to change your own commitments, goals, and values through new behaviors if you feel plateaued and unhappy. Doing something, even if you think it is minor, is vastly more effective than simply understanding what's going on.

Your attitude will change when you change what you are doing. Your goal is to feel good about what you are doing.
4. *Model* being a satisfied, committed, and productive person who knows she is valuable to the organization. Your goal is to set an example of a structurally plateaued person who is neither content plateaued nor plateaued in life.

As leaders of plateaued people, managers have to move beyond resigned acceptance to being models of satisfied and productive people. Those who have already plateaued really need to develop new ideas about what success involves and to believe they are successful. Mostly, they need to believe that being structurally plateaued can become the stimulus to creating the next and different phase of a rich life. When managers are convinced that being plateaued can become the opportunity to set and achieve new goals and expand the whole of life, then they are in a position to be effective leaders of their plateaued subordinates.

Counsel People

In most organizations, managers are told that one of their most important responsibilities is to counsel their people. Subordinates say they value being counseled enormously. They see it as a significant gift of a busy manager's time, one that says that the manager is seriously interested in how they're doing. Managers say that counseling subordinates is one of the most significant things they can do. But they usually don't do it.

The main reason managers avoid counseling is they don't feel they have the skills to do it. Basically, they don't know how to handle emotional encounters, especially when they involve issues beyond those of work. I've taught managers how to counsel in as little as half a day. It's helpful if you don't think of it as standing in the shoes of a professional, but rather as an attitude and a set of behaviors that you bring to conversations that involve important and personal issues.

At work, most people would really prefer to keep things cool, to stay away from the personal and certainly from the emotional. But issues like plateauing, which involve everything important to people, may well affect work performance. Most managers don't want to counsel, in the sense that they don't want to tell people what to do in their life. That's how they should feel and, in fact, they shouldn't do it. Managers have the responsibility to tell people what to do in terms of work. Managers do not have the right or the responsibility to tell people what to do with their lives.

A manager is not a counselor and should not try to be one. But a manager should be able to counsel. That simply means that a manager should be comfortable *as a listener* when issues are personal. People need counseling because they need to talk about problems that originate at work, or those that arise outside but affect their work, and they need to understand where they stand.

Your objective is that people's behavior at work change. But *you* don't change their behavior, *they* do. All a manager can do it to help others gain awareness so they can choose to change what they do. You cannot solve other people's problems, but by listening keenly and asking questions, you can help them see things more clearly. That puts them in a better position to choose options that they hadn't seen before.

When you counsel, don't decide beforehand what the issues are and what the solutions should be. Instead of making judgments, maintain an open attitude. That means listening so well and so hard that you ask excellent questions in response to what the other person is saying. You are not the subject of the conversation—the other person is.

You want to learn about the other person, but more than that, you want him to learn about himself as he answers your questions. You signal your genuine interest and concern by your response to what he says. *Most of the time, you are not telling, you're asking. And then you listen.* Your questions don't have to be profound or penetrating. An effective question often involves nothing more than a restatement of what someone just said plus a long pause while you wait for him to respond. People, like nature, abhor a vacuum. If you just wait, they will fill the silence.

You want to ask good enough questions that people feel relieved because they've disclosed what's bothering them. Then the real issues becomes clearer to you, and to them. Since the issue is not your problem, you should be able to keep your psychological distance, and that will allow you to see choices that they are too close to perceive.

They may ask you for advice. In general, the best strategy is not to give it. You can say, "I appreciate your confidence in me, but let's take some time and see what options are available. What choices have you been thinking about?" *Don't solve their problems. Instead, emphasize their choices.* You can ask, "What are you going to do? What do you think will happen if you make that choice?" Unlike coaching at work, in counseling about life, we try to avoid telling people what to do.

Also, you don't necessarily have to agree with them. Your responsibility, your role is to be an empathic, sensitive listener. If you disagree, that's okay, as long as you don't get emotionally involved. You can manage their becoming emotional if you keep your distance and observe emotions as behavior that you want to ask questions about. Emotional responses are data, and you are better off with more rather than less information.

You can deal with an emotion that is on the table, but you cannot deal with one that is hidden. It will fester and grow larger. Try saying, "You seem to be upset. This is what I think you were saying. Is that what you said?" It's as simple as that. If you do feel inadequate in the situation, you should suggest they talk with a professional. You might say, "I'm feeling uncomfortable here. I think it might be a good idea if you went to talk with someone whose business is listening."

Counseling is valuable because talking about what's really bothering us is helpful in itself. Counseling is also helpful because when a manager gives someone time and full attention, that says, "You are important to me." Counseling is useful as a way of gaining perspective so that people are helped to move toward solving their problems. Very basically, people like to talk about themselves with someone who is not judging them, is not telling them what to do, and really concentrates on what they're saying. As a result of counseling, people can feel better and gain the sense that they can make decisions that are good for them.

Eliminate Content Plateauing

Eliminating content plateauing does not solve the issues raised by structural plateauing; that always requires facing that reality. But changing people's responsibilities does address the need for challenge and the sense of alienation that comes when people feel taken for granted. The earlier onset of structural plateauing increases the emphasis on content plateauing and on its solution: satisfaction and success through mastering new work.

Organizations can use lateral transfers to alleviate the stress of content plateauing. In addition to the stimulation that such transfers generate, those job changes also assure people that the organization is confident they can handle different responsibilities. *While people really want the affirmation of a promotion, they will feel good about a lateral transfer if there is challenge, and their new responsibilities are important.* Although changing people's jobs always involves some loss of productivity while the new tasks are being mastered, the possibility of significantly increasing their involvement because of new challenges far outweighs this loss.

Managers can create many more job changes if they think about positions abstractly, as a collection of responsibilities that can be combined in different ways. In addition to changing people from one existing position to another, managers can exchange some responsibilities between people who remain in their job. These exchanges can take place at the same grade level or between levels, if the status differences are not too great.

Lateral transfers should be thought of on three dimensions: horizontal, vertical, and in terms of time. The simplest changes are horizontal; people are transferred from one job to another. (See Figure 4.)

More complex horizontal changes involve altering jobs, creating essentially new positions by combining old and new responsibilities. (See Figure 5.)

Another technique that is also horizontal is job "clustering," where several people in related positions are grouped together. (See Figure 6.) Each has some specific, permanent responsibilities,

Figure 4.   Simple horizontal transfers.

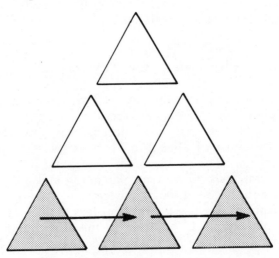

Figure 5. Complex horizontal transfers.

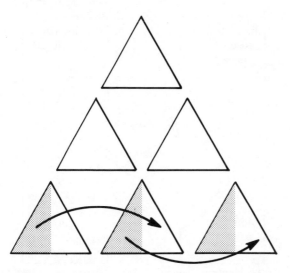

and they all share work from a common pool. In the general pool of responsibilities, the tasks remain pretty much the same but, like the pieces in a kaleidoscope, they get redistributed every so often, so that everyone gets a reasonably continual infusion of newness. Of course in this system the manager has to be alert for duplication of effort and for its opposite: tasks remaining undone.

If the difference between grades is not too great, more elaborate changes can be made, shifting some responsibilities vertically as well as horizontally. (See Figure 7.) If possible, a task reassignment from a lower grade should be balanced by one from a higher grade. It should be made clear that this does not involve either a promotion or a demotion but is, instead, intended to avoid content plateauing.

Managers can create job changes by exchanging people with other managers. Many managers assume that's not possible because other units will only be interested in taking a "star," the person a manager is most reluctant to give up. But since *every* manager has the problem of creating challenge for competent plateaued people, an exchange is advantageous for everyone.

The third variable is time. Horizontal or vertical changes can vary from short-term assignments to permanent new positions. One of the most flattering changes is a short-term assignment *if* the person is relieved of some of her regular duties. In that case, a

Figure 6.   Job clustering.

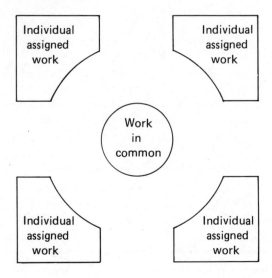

manager is saying, "Of all the people I have available for this important task, you are the best qualified and I select you. This job is so important that I am going to relieve you of some of your regular work so you can really give it your attention." If you don't relieve her of some of her regular work, instead of being a flattering reward, the special assignment can feel like just another burden on the back of the donkey.

Business could also borrow an idea from universities. Faculty members, who are hired for their professional expertise, move into administration or management for a specific term, often from three to five years, and then return to research and teaching. People who are technically expert often move into managing other technical experts, and back. While it may require a period of education to become technically expert again, this kind of move can generate a period of creativity.

Another effective technique is to organize people into work teams. Since members of a team have both common and unique skills, the group can handle a broader range of projects than can that same number of individuals working separately. Working in a team is a way to increase the amount of change in the content of what all the group members do. If team members cut across functions such as product development, finance, and marketing,

Figure 7. Vertical and horizontal transfers.

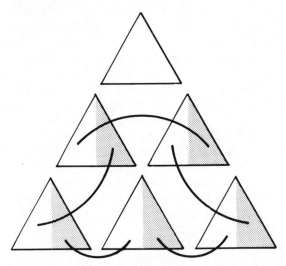

then to some degree all members will have to address the full range of problems rather than their narrow speciality.

Let People Know You Know They're There

Managers have to pay attention to people. In the office, attention frequently takes the form of comments about people's performance. While feedback about the work they're doing is specific to work, it is, at the same time, a communication that you know they're there. In the landmark Western Electric Hawthorne studies where productivity rose no matter what test conditions management imposed, the lesson was that giving people feedback, telling them that you know what they're doing, usually evokes a positive response, even if the feedback itself is negative. People are hungry for some indication that others care enough to notice them. It's hard to imagine anything worse than being ignored.

In contrast with counseling, which deals with the long term and the personal and is not judgmental, feedback involves the relative short term and is an evaluation of performance. When you give feedback, you tell people exactly what they're doing well and should continue doing, and specifically what they're not doing well and how it could be improved.

It's an apple pie observation, an obvious truism, that people want positive feedback. Of course they do. What is surprising is that they want *negative* feedback, too. Sometimes managers get angry when I say that. It's because they think of negative feedback as hostile criticism. Hostile criticism always creates resentment and resistance; that's not what I mean at all. Good negative feedback does not refer to the person, only to what he does, and it makes explicit suggestions for doing better. It's forthright and honest but it is never hostile. There is no attempt to belittle the other person. While the explicit message is that this behavior could be better, the implicit message is that the person is good enough to improve. In this sense negative feedback is reassuring, because it tells him how well he's doing, specifies the areas that could be bettered, and provides guidelines for the improvement.

When negative feedback is given in a nonhostile, specific, and constructive way, the subordinate should experience it as input from someone who cares about the quality of his work. It is a message from a manager to an employee that says, "Even though I am really busy, I keep an eye on you and the work you're doing. You, as a person, and the responsibilities you have, are important enough to me that I'm aware of what's going on with you. I know what you're capable of doing and I'll help you by telling you what you've done unusually well and what I think could be improved."

People feel resentful when they don't get the positive feedback they believe they've earned, and they feel anxious when there is no negative feedback. We all know we're not perfect. We're aware that we do not complete every assignment equally well or as well as we can. Therefore, when a manager doesn't say, "This is not up to your usual standards," the absence of criticism casts doubt on any praise. A few negative observations increase the value of the positive ones. If the manager *really* knows what someone is doing, sometimes the observations must be negative.

Since negative feedback has much more emotional impact than positive feedback, it should be used sparingly. The desirable proportions are lots of praise and only a little criticism.

Create New Rewards

When I ask managers to define "rewards," they usually say promotions and money. Those are the great rewards, but not the only ones. The danger is that if managers consider them the only rewards, then when they don't have them to give, they don't reward at all. When people are working hard, they need to be rewarded. Frequently.

Anything can become a reward if it's something that people compete for, earn, and value. Because you cannot always reward with money or promotion, you have to think about the various assets you have and designate some of them as rewards.

You have to be creative in constructing rewards. There's a limit to how many new titles, bonuses, office furnishings, or choice office locations you can provide. Some rewards are the opportunity to have fun, especially a vacation. Some rewards can meet people's intrinsic needs, such as the opportunity to do different work or return to school. Becoming a leader of a task force or participating in an outside conference can be a form of recognition. Leading an in-house seminar is an especially effective reward for technical professionals. If the organization has a policy of giving sabbaticals, people can compete for them. Then their reward is the opportunity to teach or work in a government or community agency—or to not work at all.

Some of the best rewards are symbolic, constructed to be of emotional importance to the recipients. Two of the cleverest rewards I know of were devised by one very smart general manager. He gave all his staff members an extravagantly expensive attaché case, which said they were of great value to him, and a portable phone, which said he could not afford to be out of touch with them.

Managers can increase the number of *symbols* of recognition, which makes it possible for employees in every kind of job to earn recognition. When you deal with large issues, it's easy to underestimate the reward value of ceremonies or symbols. The specific form of recognition is much less important than the reward of being singled out—an article in a house magazine, a photograph with the CEO, a compliment spoken loudly enough that other people hear it. The purpose of the reward is to convey the message that no matter the size of the organization, individuals are noticed, and whether they are fast-track or plateaued, their contributions are needed and valued.

Encourage Initiative

The most significant symptom of distress in plateaued people—because it is the most destructive—is their passivity. As they withdraw and become uninvolved with people and work, nothing good happens for them and they exist in a chronic low-level depression. That symptom is particularly important because their passivity increases their sense of powerlessness. They don't initiate changes in what is happening to them, so they lose more self-esteem and the courage to try. Feeling powerless is a core reason for their alienation.

While managers can encourage employees to create initiatives for themselves in any sphere of life, the most relevant area is their work. The objective is to replace the feeling of being acted upon with the feeling of being the actor. As employees experience success in creating options, taking the initiative, and making decisions, they gain greater confidence. The process of creating improvement for oneself is reinforced by success in doing it. That gain in confidence is maximized when the idea for change comes from the employee, rather than the manager.

Very simply and literally, managers should *require* their employees to make suggestions about how their skills could be better used in their current jobs or future ones. While not all ideas can be accomplished nor all suggestions accepted, managers should say, "Tell me what you want to do and figure out if it can be done."

Overall, the objective is to replace passivity with activity in which the person is responsible for the initiatives they create. Activity generates a sense of mastery and optimism, as long as some change does happen.

One indirect but powerful way that managers can increase people's initiative and sense of personal power is by creating work teams. Every member of a team is expected to contribute and lead. Managers often think they use a team format, but most of the time that's not true. What they're really doing is creating a group in which the original hierarchy continues. Members of the group may voice opinions, but everyone knows that the final decision will actually be made by the group leader. As a result, everyone talks to the leader, and many will not talk at all until they know where the leader is going.

A team is fundamentally different: power is redistributed so that everyone has an equal voice. The leader has to minimize the power of the leader's role so that everyone participates in initiating ideas and making decisions. Every member is considered responsible for having an opinion and is required to give it. Decisions are reached by consensus. In a team, all members are peers.

Effective team leaders empower the members and hold them accountable for participation. The only way you get everyone to be active is to require participation in making decisions and then hold people accountable for the quality of the decision. The assumption that everyone will initiate and decide then becomes a group norm. Peer pressure encourages full participation by everyone. In other words, in an effective team, no one is allowed to be passive or silent. When the team is successful, everyone will feel powerful, participatory, and accountable. This is a powerful technique for eliciting commitment, creating contributors rather than adversaries, and increasing initiation and participation. It is, therefore, a powerful technique for dealing with some of the secondary effects of being structurally plateaued.

Discourage a Workaholic Life

A workaholic is an asset in the short term for the organization and a liability in the long run. Workaholics are often unusually productive as long as the system pays off. But when promotions end, these people, who desperately need success, suffer severely. No institution can provide all the sources for self-esteem for anyone for very long.

The most common symptom of distress in plateaued people is that they increase the amount of time they work, but they do not work well. When further success is not achieved, they continue to increase the hours they work because they don't know what else to do with themselves. But the workaholic life made them especially vulnerable in the first place. Continuing that lifestyle only increases their vulnerability: they don't work productively and they don't achieve success. Over time, their depression increases.

Managers usually don't encourage a workaholic life directly; they don't tell people that they should work 70 hours a week. But they do encourage it indirectly when they criticize those who work 40 hours a week. Emphasis should be on what is produced and not on how long it took.

While conversations in the office normally begin with the subject of work, if the issue is plateauing, there's a good chance that the topic will broaden into more personal and emotional concerns that involve the quality of someone's life. If the plateaued person is a workaholic, he or she may need encouragement in changing the commitment balance. While managers should not probe into someone's personal life, and they should not tell someone what to do with life, they can listen and counsel and suggest.

It is appropriate for managers to encourage people to identify options that will create more satisfying lives. Managers can ask employees if they've considered participating in community organizations, or whether they've thought about doing more athletic activities, or whether they give enough time to their family or friends. When people broaden their lives, they protect themselves from the vulnerability of having only one source of self-esteem. From the manager's point of view, when people enlarge their commitments, the organization is protected from demands it can never meet.

Give Honest Appraisals

Performance appraisal systems are usually okay—it's the use of them that's not. Overall, everyone gets too good a report card. Performance appraisals are almost always skewed to the positive. Specifically, most people receive consistent check marks in the second-best category, the one that says they're wonderful but not quite spectacular. There are human and political reasons that cause managers to minimize the negative, but the coinage of praise ultimately becomes debased. While minimizing the negative feels nice at first, over time that is destructive to employees, because expectations about their careers have to be in line with the real evaluations of those who determine what will happen to them.

To reduce the negative effects of plateauing, it's crucial that there be as little discrepancy as possible between the employee's expectations and the manager's judgments. When appraisals are inflated, inaccurate self-evaluations and expectations will develop, then people with excessively high evaluations of ability are very likely to be traumatized when they're plateaued. Morale is highest where evaluations are tough, because that allows all employees to know where they really stand. Evading the truth usually creates feelings of mistrust, and adds to people's long-term uncertainty about their promotion probabilities. Knowledge reduces anxiety. In general, honesty is the best policy.

Employees frequently don't "know" that they're plateaued, because no superior has told them. But in another sense they do know. After all, they are aware that despite positive appraisals they're not getting promoted but other people are. People do better facing specific problems than vague fears. It is easier to get over the specific disappointment of being structurally plateaued than it is to tolerate not knowing what your competitive status is.

Should a manager tell people they are probably structurally plateaued? That's a judgment call. In my opinion, if someone asks you, tell the truth as you see it. If someone is probably plateaued, is continuing to work well, appears involved and satisfied, and does not raise the issue, don't say anything. If, on the other hand, a plateaued employee has become unproductive, appears dissatisfied, and is showing symptoms of distress, a manager *should* raise the issue. If the employee says, "Yes, I'm wondering what's going on," the manager should candidly discuss this employee's relative status and current prospects.

Managers owe employees their honest perception of the employees standing. But you also owe them their dignity. When you tell people that you believe that their chances for promotion are small, you should also direct their attention to the work satisfactions and achievements they will be able to get. Take the conversation to spheres of work and life in which they can win. While telling the truth, you can also create a mood that is positive, forward-looking, and constructive.

Manage by "Walking Around"

In the most effective organizations, those who lead are accessible to those who are led. That is a basis for the sense of "we" rather than an emphasis on "me." While the achievements of an individual are finite, those of the whole organization are unlimited. It is always desirable to create an identification with the organization and with all its accomplishments.

More specific to plateauing, managers who have continuous, informal, spontaneous exchanges with those who work for them are creating the opportunity for honesty, for counseling, for the reassurance that you know employees exist and that you care.

When managers are continuously and informally accessible, people are less likely to feel powerless and insignificant; they know they can reach you and talk with you. With informal access, the level of spontaneous interaction increases, especially between bosses and those they manage.

The most effective managers are able to mobilize more people to get things done. They "encourage, cajole, praise, reward, demand, manipulate, and generally motivate others with great skill in face-to-face situations."[33] They rely a great deal on indirect influence, and they achieve that by spending a lot of time with people. That style of management makes subordinates feel powerful and significant, because they can talk to those with the power to make things happen.

Some Final Comments

Managers have an enormous amount of influence on those they manage. They have the responsibility, and should create the opportunity, to help employees realize that plateauing is a solvable problem and one that can be dealt with openly. Life offers many opportunities for a person to exert personal style and enhance self-worth without being dependent on reaching the top rung of the organizational ladder.

Managers can reduce people's negative feelings about themselves and the organization by helping them to understand the phenomenon of plateauing. You can relieve them of any sense they have failed. You can reduce their anxiety by telling them how you really evaluate them, and by providing both positive and negative feedback. You can challenge people by giving them new responsibilities, which tells them you have confidence in their abilities. You can encourage them to broaden their lives. In all these efforts, you are addressing the issue of plateauing; more than that, you are telling people they are significant and valuable.

Your goal as a manager is to help plateaued people become and remain reenergized so they are effective contributors. You will be much more effective in those efforts if you truly feel that there *are* other worthwhile goals besides promotion. To be most effective with plateaued employees, you have to believe that when people stop pursuing a narrow and traditional definition of success, they are in a much better position to find profound satisfactions in a broader life.

When people reach the end of their promotion ladder, they need to stop chasing a goal they will no longer catch. Until they do, they feel frustrated and emotionally depleted. It is much easier for people to give up their old ambitions when it is clear that there are other valuable goals they can catch. Managers have a great deal of impact in enabling people to esteem new and different goals, in enabling people to be able to say, "I like my job and I do it well. I'm okay where I am and I'm satisfied. I'm willing to work hard but work's not going to run my life any more because I've got some other things I need to do."

When plateaued people define new kinds of achievements for themselves, they find gratifications in their present and excitement in their future. When that happens, everyone benefits.

11

Change Your Work and Create a Future

Death, taxes, and structural plateauing—those are the only things you can be sure of. Content plateauing and plateauing in life are not far behind. While, ideally, we'd all like to manage our careers so we plateau at the same time we retire, few of us achieve that. Whatever the form it takes, feeling plateaued can force us to face the question of what we're going to do for the rest of our lives.

The facts tell us that plateauing in our work and in our lives is normal and happens to almost everyone. But, while that is useful information and a comforting perspective, it doesn't lessen the importance of the problem or the crucial need to do something about it. I'm going to discuss the core psychological tasks involved, the factors that face all who set out to *really* change the work they do. Since individuals and occupations are so varied, the mechanics of specific change are left up to you.

In terms of structural plateauing, you have to change your aspirations. In terms of content plateauing, you have to change some aspect of the work you do. In terms of plateauing in life, you have to change your capacity to experience, some of your priorities, and some of the ways that you live.

In general, you need to:

- *Be willing for change to happen.* This means you don't resist change, don't insist on clinging to the ways things have always been.
- *Motivate yourself.* This means you are willing to create and engage in the difficult first steps of change.

- *Create new ambitions.* This means you admit that the old ones are no longer assets.
- *Accept the risks.* This means you are willing to take on some amount of uncertainty.
- *Be disciplined.* This means you do not allow yourself the illusory comfort of being passive; you are willing to face the issues actively.
- *Let go of past habits.* This means you acknowledge that while those styles created gains, they also incurred profound costs.
- *Be compassionate.* This means you acknowledge that as you change, you are less predictable to others. You have the responsibility of communicating what you are trying to do, and of listening to those who are affected by your efforts.
- *Be patient.* This means you remember that the transition phases in life ordinarily take four to five years, because changing in basic ways is hard.

Two Who Did It

Russ and Alice are one of my favorite examples of people who successfully made the changes they needed to. I like their story because it so clearly demonstrates the courage of "ordinary" people.

Not long ago my husband and I decided to take a few days off and spend the weekend with friends in Santa Barbara. Our friends offered to make the hotel arrangements and called to say they'd made reservations at a brand-new bed and breakfast place they were sure we'd love. My enthusiasm was underwhelming: I don't like required togetherness with people I don't know. But I decided not to protest.

When we arrived at the inn, the door was opened by our host, who introduced himself as Russ and welcomed us to his home. And a lovely home it was. The living room was beautiful and livable, an exquisite combination of shape, color and texture; everything combined to make visitors feel good. There were eight guest rooms; each was different and each was perfect. I wondered if the owners were professional decorators. Eventually I asked them how they'd come to have a bed and breakfast hotel, and they told me their story.

After their kids left home, Russ and Alice had spent several years wondering what they were going to do with themselves. He'd been in retail trade all his life, starting as a shoe salesman, then manager, and ultimately the owner of a shoe store. She was a secretary, and at one time or another had worked in law, medical, and corporate executive offices. Starting some time in their mid-forties they simply decided they didn't want to continue doing what they were doing. The only thing they knew was that they weren't going to spend the rest of their lives the same old way. It wasn't that life was terrible, it just wasn't exciting—there was no challenge in it, so there was no creativity.

Like most people, they weren't really aware of how repetitive their lives had become until all the children left home. As long as children are home it's easy to get psychologically involved with what they're doing; their lives change, so yours seems to change also. Once Alice and Russ realized their lives had slid into comfortable boredom, they agreed to do something about it, but they didn't know what.

For several years, they thought up various ideas and tried to develop plans to make them happen. But while some of the ideas sounded good, none seemed just right. In frustration, they went on vacation to the British Isles and wandered around for a month. They sometimes stayed at bed and breakfast places, which are widespread there. They came back home, refreshed and happy, totally unaware they'd subconsciously gotten the idea they were looking for.

The need to come up with a scheme and make plans became a nagging constant. Then one day, for no particular reason, one of them mentioned having a bed and breakfast place. They looked at each other—bingo! For the first time, a possible choice sounded good *and* felt good. They would work together, it would be something they could share, they liked people, and they enjoyed entertaining. It would be such a big change that it would be hard. They'd really be starting all over. But that, in fact, was exactly what they were looking for.

Once they had the sense that they knew what they wanted, the rest was relatively easy. They read, they talked to people, and they visited possible sites. They've been open for six months now and they've learned a lot. Of course they're still learning. They're also working 15 hours a day and that's okay with them. Alice and Russ have moved off their work plateau and their life plateau. While it's a little scary, mostly it's exciting. In a total way, they're revitalized.

Taking the Initiative

Whether you stay in your current organization or move, whether you work in a hierarchical organization or are self-employed, don't allow yourself to be passive. *You must take the initiative in making change happen.*

If you don't take the initiative but wait around for superiors or fate to create opportunities, you increase your sense of being powerless. Your lack of activity does, in fact, give others too much power over what happens to you. Plateaued people often tell me, "I do my job and I just hope that something will turn up." Feeling powerless, they create the circumstances that increase their powerlessness and their vulnerability to stress.[48] People who work in large organizations seem especially prone to being "good," to waiting for the good fairy to notice them and reach out with a magic wand.

A 36-year-old engineer at a major *Fortune* 500 company told me he'd been waiting five years for the first promotion to management. I asked him what he would say to his superiors to justify giving him more responsibilities. He said he hadn't thought about it because it wasn't in his power to make it happen. I suggested that in a competitive situation it's not enough to do good work and hope you're noticed. You have to make the case for yourself; if you can't, that in itself says a lot.

It's your responsibility to tell the people with power what you want. You know your area of work and your competencies better than anyone else. You have to think about what changes are possible or not possible. You have to strategize for success and prepare for disappointment. You also need contingency plans.

As you seek to change the work you do, or the place in which you do it, or its importance in your life, you need to know what you want and how you feel. Are you satisfied with the work you are doing and the organization where you do it, or unsatisfied? Do you feel challenged in work and other parts of your life, or do you need more challenge? If so, where might you get it? Is there a time frame in which you're thinking of change? How will you feel if that change does not occur? What will you do? You have to get the facts about yourself from *you*. Then you can think about options. While there is never a guarantee that you can change the content of your assignments or get a promotion, the worst case is to have to say to yourself, "I didn't try and it didn't happen."

You gain some sense of control just because you think things through. *Nobody thinks about you as much as you do?* So you have to do as much of the thinking and initiating for yourself as you can. You are in a unique position to make a case for yourself, to initiate the redesign of your work so that it's more interesting and challenging. No one knows your job, your skills, your aptitudes, and your interests as well as you do.

In order to create opportunity you have to define your work as broadly as possible, understand how your work contributes to something important, and strategize so that more of your work contributes to significant goals. Think about the aspects of your work that give you intrinsic satisfactions, and enlarge them. Then speak up, and ask for a change.

A lateral transfer—the opportunity to do new work that does not involve a promotion and is not a preparation for a promotion— is a valuable and available way to create change. Even a demotion can be regarded as an opportunity if the work will be satisfying and challenging and your salary remains the same. The sense of opportunity in such a move is the result of replacing the insistent self-demand for unavailable promotion with the strong desire to be more professional, more expert, but in something new.

While you are unlikely to get everything you want when you do initiate recommendations, you are more likely to get *something* than if you do nothing. Besides, even if you try and fail, you have gained confidence from actively initiating, and that confidence will make it easier for you to keep initiating until you get work that is more satisfying.

Changing Organizations, Changing Careers

I'm often asked if the solution for people who are plateaued at work is to change organizations. My answer is, "Sometimes." There are always situations where people are blocked by factors specific to them—their organization or department is static or in decline but their field is growing, or their manager is a slot-stopper but too young to retire, or the chemistry is bad with their boss. In those circumstances, changing where they work and whom they work for is a good idea. It's hardly surprising that people achieve much more success when they leave a situation where they were stymied and blocked.

But structural plateauing will get you in the end. If you

imagine all the organizations in the country lined up between here and the horizon, you will notice that despite differences in the width of their base or in the stretch of their height, they all have the same general shape—they're all pyramids. They all fall under the Rule of 99%. If you change organizations, you may rise higher and delay structural plateauing, but unless you are very exceptional, you'll eventually reach a level beyond which you will not climb. You never escape the long-term need to accept that.

But what about changing careers altogether? A second career means more than a change of organizations; just changing where you work can mean doing old work in a new place. A real second career is a major throw of the dice. But for those who can accept the risk, it may be the best of all options. Since a second career usually involves beginning again in midcareer, at midlife, goals of promotion and of rising to the top are usually insignificant simply because you're starting so late. So it's relatively easy for the central ambition of a second career to be that of enjoying the mind-stretching, rejuvenating exercise of great challenge.

Some people, like me, have knowledge and skills that can be transferred and sold in a different way. Often, though, to be realistically possible, a second career requires a major investment in capital, education, and experience. If you begin again, you have to be prepared for a loss of economic security, at least for a while, and for a very likely loss of status. You have to really believe that you will ultimately gain more than you'll lose, if only because you already know you do not want to do what you're doing for the rest of your working life.

A second career is a very exciting strategy for getting off a plateau—but it is also very scary. I've therefore come to the conclusion that you have to *focus on where to begin and not on what you will become.* I mean that you must take steps to start the change. Of course you have to think a lot about what your real goals are and what your options might be. You do have to read and talk to people and feel your way. But many people get so involved in the introspection of how they feel, or in analyses of what might happen, that nothing happens. They don't do anything. You may *decide not to change* occupations, but that is intrinsically different from not doing anything because you don't decide. A key to well-being is not being passive.

When I talk with people who are thinking about changing what they do and ask them what they like to do, they usually tell me what they'd next like to do in work. The question of what you like to *do* is not the same as what would you like to do *in work*. The first question is much more general than the second, and that's important; if you ask yourself a narrow question, you restrict the alternatives you can see.

For example, I asked a plateaued executive vice president of a *Fortune* 500 company what he liked to do. He said, "I'd like to buy a company in the division I run and manage that company for myself." In terms of the next phase of his career, he might end up deciding to do exactly that, but he really needs to think about it differently.

After a few minutes he said, "I think what I like most of all is writing. There's a lot of pleasure even in writing a perfect business letter or memo. I save my best ones and every once in a while I go back and read them." Thinking about what he *really* liked to do, he started remembering essays he'd written a long time ago when he was traveling all over the world. He hadn't thought about them for years, but as he started to recall the circumstances in which he'd written them, he got increasingly excited. Then he said, "It would be a pity if I went to my grave and never tried to write that novel."

I don't know whether he'll write a novel and neither does he. But now that he is aware of the idea, he might. He might also decide to buy a company and run it. But if he does, it will be because he came to the conclusion that of *all* the things he likes to do, running a company is the one he enjoys the most.

When you start to think about a second career, the only thing you can be sure of is that you're dissatisfied doing what you're now doing. All else is speculation. You cannot know where a change will take you. Usually, in the beginning of the process of change, all you have is a vague desire, a general objective, and a fair amount of fear. The anxiety will reduce when you begin to see more specific goals and the initial strategies that will move you toward them. You have to be ready to cope with the opportunities that don't happen despite your efforts and to use the opportunities that arise unpredictably.

When you strategize to change careers, you need to create several different routes or options to get you where you want to go. For one thing, you'll have to contend with the vagaries of fate. For another, if you're moving into an occupation where you don't have the credentials or the contacts you used to, you have much less control than when you were a member of the occupational establishment. Even if you don't really have much control in the situation, a range of options makes it feel like you do.

The second careers that have a chance of being successful and providing satisfaction are usually evolutionary: they develop from an interest and knowledge you already have. If you want to begin a second career, you have to give up illusions and do a hard-nosed assay of your assets. What can you do, or what do you know, that people will want to buy from you?

A lot of the time, people want a second career because they want to work for goals that have become philosophically important but are unachievable in their old occupation. But goals based on ethics have a tendency to remain formless, as vague longings. To make a career, they have to be transformed into something specific.

A middle-aged man came to see me because after a year of reading and talking, he still didn't know what he wanted to do. He was certain that he didn't want to go back to his old work of managing a hotel. For a long time he wanted to do some kind of work that helped people achieve a sense of personal growth. But he didn't have a single credential in that occupation. On the other hand, he had instituted policies and procedures for his employees that were based on participative management. He not only ran a financially successful hotel, he ran a happy one.

I suggested that we examine his general aversion to the hotel business, and he agreed that there was nothing intrinsically terrible about hotels or the people who work in them. It was important to get that clear, because *the only thing he knew and had to sell was his experience in that business.* In other words, since he really had no other skills or experience, the first step toward a second career would involve either a significant amount of retraining or using the information he already had in a more satisfying way. I asked if he knew any people who were consultants to hotels. Yes he did; in fact he'd used them. Consultants, of course, deal with interpersonal relations, participative management, and psychological growth. I suggested that he think about working as a consultant in the hotel business, beginning as a staff person with an established consulting firm, giving them his expertise and taking from them the knowledge he needs.

This is the kind of thinking you have to do. Goals that were vague have to become specific, strategies that maximize your strengths have to be devised, and thinking has to give way to plans of action. I can't know whether this man would be hired by a consulting firm and be happy as a consultant. But until he makes a move, talks to firms, tries it out, he can't know either.

My feeling is that *your relationship to risk is probably the single most important factor in determining whether or not you should try a mega-beginning in middle age.* You may not be as satisfied in your work or your life as you want, and you may even be significantly dissatisfied, but you are unlikely to change what you do if your fears of change are greater than your desire to change.

You have to respect and accept your basic relationship to risk. You have to know whether you love it or hate it. If you are much more inclined toward security than excitement, know yourself and let that be okay with you. But if there is something important missing from your work and your life, and you are willing to put in more time and energy before you achieve success, and you are willing to accept the broad and basic risks involved, then try something new, even something very new. Go for it, because too much of life is dead if work is dull, unsatisfying, and frustrating.

Learning Is the Key to Challenge

Continuous learning is what you need for continuous challenge. When you have new information, you are more likely to be given the opportunity of doing new work.

You can learn on the job or you can go to school; you can learn specific to work and you can learn for learning's own sake. You have to decide why you want to learn and therefore what you wish to learn. Only you can decide whether your interests are shifting from one field to another, or from research to application, or from design to management, or from management back to the profession. You are the only one who can know whether you still feel creative or whether you've been on the same road so long there are deep ruts in it.

Continuous education, whether offered within corporations or in university extension divisions, has become a huge industry. The great schools of business, for example, have enormous extension catalogs of courses for postgraduates who want to upgrade and extend their skills. Courses in engineering, computers, communication technologies, management, leadership are everywhere. In its most obvious aspects, that's education to stay abreast and qualify for advancement.

Whether your organization makes it easy or hard, you have the burden of continuing your own education. Aside from the specifics learned in formal courses, you have a more basic reason to make a commitment to and to initiate your self-education. We all know that the pace of change in work is continuously accelerating. The laurel wreath of opportunity will be gained by people whose capacity to learn, whose ability to adapt and anticipate, keeps apace. You have to understand as well as know; and learning like any other skill, takes practice.

Using Your Skills in a Different Way

Plateaued people who may be unable to change their jobs need to use their knowledge and skills in different ways that feel significant. Many who are productive and satisfied are often mentors to younger people in the organization, internal consultants, and community leaders. They have found additional ways to contribute, expand their experience, and gain meaning. It is not accidental that most of the time their activities involve a larger purpose than increasing their own welfare.

Individuals need mentors and organizations need them. Guiding, supporting, leading, and training the next generation are as important at work as in the family. And, as in the family, that responsibility is best borne by those who are most mature and knowledgeable. We need to recognize the mentor as an extremely valuable organizational resource.

Only mature people can be mentors. You can't be playing "King of the Hill," competing with, jealous of, and resenting younger people when your responsibility is to bring them along. You can't be a mentor if your competitiveness leads you to perceive younger people as adversaries so that every time they succeed, you feel like you lost. Successful mentors have grown up; they've accepted their personal limits and the limits of their opportunities. Not stuck in old dreams, they've moved into the future.

If we're honest with ourselves, we admit there's always some pain when we go from seeing ourselves as a younger person's superior to watching them become a peer. There is a time of transition we have to work through, so we can experience their growing capacities as a progress that gives us pleasure. We cannot develop others until we give up the rivalry that stems from our need to see ourselves as ever youthful. In business, where there is such a premium on youth, it is difficult for anyone, but especially for men, to see the unconscious battle we wage with subordinates, sometimes wishing them to succeed and sometimes willing them to fail.[33]

Mentoring involves the challenge of being the wise teacher. The psychological task for the plateaued middle-aged person is to perceive ways in which being a mentor is advantageous to them. Middle age is more likely to be a period of personal renaissance if you facilitate the creativity and growth of younger people. Then, as they win and you've helped, you're winning too.[33] When you can share in the development and success of those you have nurtured, you give up a lonely and ultimately unsuccessful competition with the next generation.[14] Enhancing your value to others in this way will enhance your value to yourself. You will have created a new way to earn self-respect and create challenge.

Another way you can create challenge, especially after you have acquired significant skills, knowledge, and credentials, is to become really involved in your community and your government. The volunteer sector can be as gratifying as your professional work if you approach it with the same kind of commitment and orientation to achieve. As with anything, a token involvement produces few gains.

In the last 15 years, business has increasingly accepted responsibility for some of our serious social concerns. Thus, more and more business people are participating as volunteers in community agencies and finding that participation meaningful.[18] Business people work in those organizations because they believe the work is important, they share the same concerns, and they have skills, honed in business, that are necessary for the achievement of the goals.

Participation in the community offers opportunities to wrestle with different issues and populations, to have hands-on experience, to be creative, to exert leadership, and to make a visible difference. It is another place where leadership and wisdom can be used.

Change the Percentage of Your Commitments

You can create change in your life by altering the percentage of time you give to your various commitments. The payoff from any commitment is proportionate to your investment in it. Roughly speaking, your psychological commitment is proportionate to the amount of time you give to something. For many, time is a very scarce commodity; when you give time, you give something that is very valuable to you and therefore to the recipient of it. If you've been wrapped up in your career, changing your commitments involves reapportioning time so more of it is given to a spouse or lover, children, friends, the community, and yourself.

Most people need to work, and they need to work hard enough at something tough enough that there is a feeling of accomplishment. I am not saying that people shouldn't work or work hard. But, especially when people plateau, it can be immensely constructive if they reallocate the time they bring to their commitments so that significant amounts of psychological energy are brought to other sectors of life than work.

You can think of this as a matter of return on investment. There's a difference in what you can gain from work when your career is ascending compared to when you are no longer moving upward. So, as the possible gains change, how much should you invest in work? What balance of priorities would help you avoid being plateaued in life when you plateau in work? I believe that for most people the percentage of time you give to the many aspects of your life should change in different life phases.

Here is a simple exercise that people often find revealing. In the circle below (Figure 8) you're going to draw a pie chart of your

Figure 8. Current time usage.

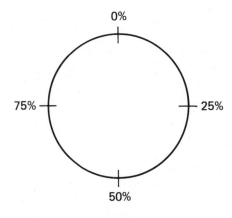

week. A week has 168 hours. Work out the percentage of time you give to:

> Work. Include commuting time and work in the evening and
>   on weekends.
> Sleep.
> Your spouse or lover without the children.
> Your children without your spouse or lover.
> The family as a whole.
> Reading that is unrelated to work.
> Hobbies.
> The arts.
> Athletics.
> The community.
> Friends.
> Time for yourself.

Now do it again *as you would like your week to be* (Figure 9). Then ask your emotional partner to do the same thing.

Some people find that work, commuting, and sleep can account for 60 to 75 percent of the hours in the week. That leaves little time for anything else and little energy with which to do it. The truth is that we're working longer hours than we used to. In 1984, the average American worked 17 percent more hours than in 1983 and had 31 percent less leisure time. Completing the pie chart often reveals that little spontaneous time is given to a

Figure 9. Ideal time usage.

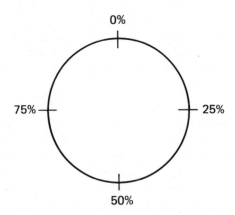

spouse, the children, or friends. Most frequent of all, people find they give little time to themselves.

Time that you take for yourself is the only uncommitted time; it's the only time that is free of roles. And it's very important. People need to carve out some time every day or every week in which they do whatever it is they need to do. More specifically, in that time you are not to feel responsible for anyone else. Self time is not selfish. It is time for your Self. You owe yourself that. Being able mentally to leave the stress of work and relax is necessary for creativity. It's simple: we have to recharge our batteries.

Peter McColough, the chairman of Xerox, says:

> I insist on taking vacations. I take vacations well above average, six or eight weeks a year—although never six or eight weeks at a crack. I always have one or two vacations scheduled beyond the next one. I sail in the summer and I ski almost every weekend in the winter. Around here it's not shameful to take a vacation; no one feels guilty about taking time off.
>
> We say over and over that we want people who are balanced—that we are not looking for workaholics. We expect our people to work hard. We also do believe that there is a broader purpose to a good corporation than just making money. We try to bring balance to people's lives. We greatly encourage them to do outside activities so they can get some interests outside of business.
>
> Despite the climate here, which still has a lot of stress, some people just can't cope with it. I would say that some of the people who left didn't lead balanced lives. Some of them had no outside interests—their lives were totally business. . . . We have had people, for example, who drank too much and took pills to make them sleep at night. They got so that they could not stand the pressure.[10]

The most importance change in terms of priorities is creating a balance between your personal and professional lives. If there is a significant imbalance, the chances are that you don't do terribly well in either sector. The pie chart tells you what you're doing now. With awareness, you can rechoose your priorities. Then your life will start being the way you want it to be.

Don't Work at Change Too Hard

Since success is usually the result of hard work, people usually work hard when they want to solve a problem. When we don't make progress, we try harder. Sometimes you can achieve more progress when you don't try so hard. Working hard means concentrating, and that means focusing on what is conscious, on what you are aware of. Your subconscious mind is a rich store of ideas you're usually not aware of, but they will come to mind if you just let go.

Working very hard and keeping very busy shuts out the subconscious and also makes it hard to feel. As you seek to change what you do, you should also be trying to broaden your capacity to experience. Therefore, you have to let yourself feel. This means that you shouldn't *work* at changing your life, keeping yourself as busy as possible. Being very busy can change from purposeful activity to busyness designed to prevent feelings. That, of course, is why people who are anxious or depressed try to fill up their time completely.

Knowing and doing are only two legs of life's tripod. The third leg is feeling. If you strive too hard, if you're very intense, it's easy to lose awareness of your feelings. A key idea in changing how you experience your life is to make sure there are periods in which you are not doing much of anything. For most people, that's very hard to do.

The objective of doing nothing is to feel everything. That's important, because people who feel plateaued in life have lost the capacity to experience very much of anything. If you're to be as fully alive and as effective in business as you can be, you need to feel your own feelings and be sensitive to the emotions of other people. If you're out of touch with emotions, frightened of feeling them and scared of expressing them, you have a lot of learning to do.

You can learn to become aware of emotion. Bartolomé suggests, for example, that the next time you come home from work and see one of your children, stop for a moment and concentrate on what you're feeling as you look at that child.[8] You may find you feel nothing, or a little bit, or a lot. Your emotions can be positive or negative, unexpected or familiar, painful or joyful. When you return to work and walk into your office, pause a moment and sense how you feel. As you interact with people at work, do you feel anything toward them? Take time to learn what your experience is and then try to verbalize the feelings.

Of course you'll also work at trying to solve your problems. This is a matter of proportion. Those who have gone through life with no awareness of their emotions gain enormously from letting themselves become aware of them. You have a better chance of gaining insight, perceiving new ideas, and being creative if you allow yourself to experience fully. You want to achieve a sense of inner direction because when you have it, your cognitive analysis will tell you your new goals are correct—and it will also *feel* right.

Most of all, you want to achieve emotional insight because that's the main way we accomplish personal change. When plateauing creates a sense of crisis, a feeling of despair or enormous fear, individual psychotherapy or couple or group therapy can be immensely helpful. People of "normal pathology," people who are not mentally sick but who are experiencing the trauma of uncertainty and change, can gain help from a therapist because it's hard to see clearly when you're upset. Some people who have long suppressed their feelings and are numb to their emotions need to talk to a therapist, someone who is immensely skilled in listening, because they need help in regaining connections with their emotions.

At one time or another, most of us need help. There's no shame attached to that. The only shame is in fleeing from the issues because, in the end, that becomes a damn shame.

Change!

The decline in opportunities for promotion, resulting from a huge number of qualified people in their thirties and an economy expanding too slowly to satisfy them, has one enormous implication: many people will need to restructure their thinking about success in work.

When you *feel* plateaued, you're disappointed, because there's a significant gap between what you expected and what you're experiencing. This means that you must change old habits of living, old values, and old ambitions because they're no longer routes to success. You have to develop new ones that can create profound satisfaction.

The goal of being promoted and acquiring power has to shift to a new emphasis: success through continued learning and the mastery of new problems. When ambition is transformed toward goals of increased knowledge and professionalism, toward meeting challenge, then success need never end.

There is no limit to problems or to what can be learned and mastered. You want to know that in your work you can use your skills and wisdom, you will have the opportunity to learn and to contribute, and your fulfillment in the present promises to extend into the future. That's all achievable, but you have to make it happen. When you have the courage to act, to make the changes you need, you will create a future for yourself.

12

Change Yourself
and Create a Future

Plateauing, especially in midlife, should result in an evaluation-transition period, a time when you look at what you have done and where you want to go next. This is the psychological work, the preparation for the transitions that will create the beginnings that become your future. Much of that process is conscious, some of it, like weighing options and feasibility, deliberate. It is, in fact, work. But the most basic process of change—the expansion of your capacity to engage and to be—is not conscious, is not deliberate, and is not work. What it requires is not being afraid. Every change, every movement into new territory, takes courage. In this case, you need the courage to become different from what you have been.

Earlier, I wrote that the middle-age crisis can be thought of as the time when there is not yet an answer to the question of "What will I do next?" Another way to say it is there is not yet an answer to the question of "Who will I be next?"

While there are limitations imposed by life's realities, many of our limitations are created by us, on us, as we become expert in selected sectors of being and doing. Those are the psychological limitations we must change. If you perceive opportunities for change only in terms of roles or changing your work, you narrow the range of options tremendously. You have to see that, over time, your capacity to experience, to perceive, to feel, *to be*, becomes limited if you live in one commitment and a few roles to the exclusion of others. Basically, your capacities are not limited to the sum of your roles. Your total reach of capacity is much broader than that.

You may change your work when you are plateaued. But that is too narrow a concept, especially if you are plateaued in life. There are other, more profound possibilities that involve changing your core Self. The most basic change is an expansion of the capacity to experience and perceive. Psychological growth becomes the basis of a much larger capacity to act.

Becoming Psychologically Complex

Plateauing in life results from the deadening of your capacity to experience. Thus, the best way to get off that plateau is to increase the range of what you can feel and commit to. When you are more complex—which is to say, less narrow—you have a vastly greater universe in which you can participate and from which you can gain important satisfactions. While becoming psychologically complex can be described in various ways, I like to think of it in terms of gender. When we are *very* traditional in our masculinity or femininity we *include* half of the commitments, responses, experiences, and perceptions that could be ours, and we *exclude* half. Becoming more complex, broader, involves bringing in the other half.

The Other Half

A normal development in both women and men, one that has been observed in many cultures, is that, typically in middle age, both sexes add to their psychological core personal qualities, goals, values, and self concepts that they previously excluded because they "belonged" to the opposite sex. Men become more accepting of their empathic, nurturant "feminine" side and women of their analytic, initiating "masculine" qualities. Women pursue their active side and men their intuitive capacities. As a result, they become vastly more complex, better able to leave any kind of plateau.

Broadening the self, which is the most profound of all the possible changes, is also the easiest. You just have to let it happen. You don't have to *work* to achieve this growth. Just don't resist it. You don't even have to change roles for this development to happen, although that does make it easier.

The more anxious you are about anything, the more you cling to the rules of conformity. If, like most of us, you were reared traditionally, it's only when you've achieved confidence that you can depart from the norms that signal to you and anyone else that you are a man or a woman. But when you are confident, you can engage in nontraditional behaviors or take on nontraditional values because you're no longer vulnerable.

This basic psychological expansion normally occurs when confidence and a clear sense of identity have been achieved. When we have accomplished the tasks that our culture requires of adult women and men, we become secure and we no longer need to constrict ourselves to traditional views of what we should be like. We are able to cross traditional gender lines and feel no less feminine or masculine. Confident, we don't have to conform to narrow rules of what we can be like. We are free to change, to experiment.

In the population of people now in their twenties and thirties we can see some who are already engaging in behaviors and holding attitudes that cross the traditional rules for the sexes. That's easier for them than for those who are now in their late thirties and older, because feminism led a great social movement toward the liberalization of those rules. Today, fewer categories of behavior or values are required or prohibited because a person is male or female. In the 1980s women who are ambitious in their careers aren't tagged unfeminine, and we don't think of men who care for their young children as unmasculine.

Some may view these younger people as committed to a life that includes varied roles. Actually, it's more valid to think of them as comfortable with a more complex psychological core than those who are older grew up with. When men, for example, are truly involved in child care, they're willing to open the boundaries of their inner self and be sensitive to their own and the child's emotions. When women pursue career ambition, they accept a self-orientation in that part of their life. When you cross a traditional gender line in terms of roles or work, you may also become more psychologically complex, because different roles foster different emotional responses and self-perceptions.

People who are psychologically complex are less likely to become plateaued in life because they have not narrowed what they do or who they become. It is, therefore, a highly desirable development in everyone.

While that evolution may be easier for younger people who

grew up in less restricted or traditional ways, anyone can achieve it. In middle age, it can involve a long and sometimes painful evaluation-transition period. But the outcome of that transition can be the most significant thing they can achieve if the result is a broad capacity to become interested, involved, engaged.

Psychological change leads to new psychological commitments, new values, new goals. Psychological change can therefore cause new behaviors. But that works both ways: behavior is also a fertile growing ground for psychological change. Attitudes change when behavior does. And behaviors change when attitudes do. You're more willing to try something, so you do it. Allowing your inner self to broaden (attitude) plus some responsible experimenting (behavior) will create mental and behavioral change that will get you off life's plateau.

When you become more complex, the natural result is that more commitments are possible, more goals naturally evolve, and more kinds of experiences can be fulfilling. Broadening your capacities enlarges your humanity—your ability to experience, to change, to mature . . . to relate within every kind of commitment you make.

Psychologically Traditional Women and Men

Even the great Freud wrote, "What do women *want?*" Which is not too surprising, since he was a man. The basic gender difference is so fundamental that I sometimes think it's a miracle that women and men ever understand each other.

Most people think of the major differences between men and women in terms of what they *do.* Traditionally, she stayed home and feathered their nest while he went forth to slay dragons and secure bacon. Today that's pretty irrelevant since 53 percent of the women are in the labor force (in some age groups, more like 70 percent). The crucial gender difference lies not nearly as much in the different roles of women and men as in how they *perceive* themselves in relation to the world. Traditional socialization results in the sexes being the opposite of each other.

Traditionally, men are socialized to be self-oriented. That means the world is experienced from the perspective that the self is the center. There is no judgment implied in that statement; self-oriented people can be psychologically healthy or unhealthy, selfish or generous. The self-oriented person relates to the world and makes decisions largely in terms of how he would be affected. The central words for him are *me, mine,* and *I*.

Traditional men are also geared toward action. They're much more concerned with what they do than how they feel. That's not too surprising since, at its extreme, male socialization permits men only two emotions, sexual passion and aggression (which they transform into competitiveness). All other emotions are considered feminine.

Psychologically traditional men, therefore, usually think in terms of doing. They strive to get a clear sense of where they want to go and what they need to *do* to get there. For them, it's largely a matter of career. A self-oriented man would say, "My self-esteem and my sense of who I am depend a lot on my work. I know that I'm a good engineer and it tickles me when I have to solve a really tough problem. It's true that I work awfully hard and it takes a lot of time away from my family. But I really like to work and, besides, there's no such thing as working too hard. I expect my wife to help me get ahead. That's fair because as I get more successful, we all live better. Work is my responsibility and my wife's behind me all the way."

Traditionally, females are socialized to be other-oriented. That means the world is experienced in terms of relationships with others. Here, too, I am not suggesting a judgment. Other-oriented people can be givers or takers, psychologically healthy or unhealthy.

The critical words for others-oriented people are *we, us,* and *ours*. They gain identity from being in relationships with valued people and achieve self-respect by helping others. As a result, they make decisions in light of how they would affect emotionally important people. Because of that awareness, they're very sensitive to feelings. In fact, females are socialized to experience all emotions—except those of sexual passion and aggression!

There is a profound consequence of traditional women's psychological emphasis on relationships. People who are self-oriented are mentally free to construct their goals in terms of themselves. People who are other-oriented are not free to make independent, long-term decisions in the same way. That's either because their partners are not yet known or because the partners' responses are always taken into consideration. Women who are psychologically traditional, who essentially view themselves within relationships, must, to some extent, keep their goals tentative and their ambitions unformed because the specifics of what they will do are so enmeshed with other people's priorities.

A traditional, other-oriented woman would say, "I feel good because I know that my husband and my children love me and I love them. I work very hard at that because it's terribly important to me. When I see that they're doing the best they can, I know that I've done a good job. I like working, but the truth is, my career's not as important as my husband's. Everyone needs me at home and that's where I belong."

Psychologically traditional people have only *one* major commitment—he has his career and she has her family. If a psychologically traditional wife is in the labor force, she regards work largely as a way to earn money that helps the family to live better. In that sense, working outside the home is identical with working within it, because both contribute to the welfare of others.

The crucial gender difference is not in what the sexes do; the basic sex difference is in the psychological stances of other-oriented and self-oriented. For women and men who are psychologically traditional, their interests and ambitions, their most basic perceptions of the world, are the reverse of each other. Those living in a world of psychological gender differences do not have the perceptual tools or the understanding that allows them to do or to feel in the other's world. They have half of the capacities they could have.

Changing Us

When people—especially middle-aged people—try to leave life's plateau, they may go through a period of extreme psychological change. They reverse all their previous values; they make no compromise. It's as though they have to flail violently because they're afraid of being sucked in deeper by the quicksand of their previous values. The nontraditional psychological stance is one in which traditional values and ways of perceiving are reversed.

Nontraditional Men and Women

Nontraditional men can be divided into two groups. One group remains self-oriented, but, unlike traditional men, they are not career ambitious. They say, "I don't want to work too hard. There's too much else to do in life." The second group becomes other-oriented; they perceive the world in terms of *us*. They are more involved in relationships than they are with their self-interests. This is a common temporary response when a man's marriage or important love relationship is threatened or ends. Frightened and depressed, for the first time he becomes aware of his deepest emotions and his need to belong and be loved.

It can be very difficult for self-oriented people, who have a lot invested in seeing themselves as strong and independent, to accept their emotional vulnerability. That's why this change in men is frequently born out of awful pain. But whether this development is created by anguish or is a gentle maturation, the gain is an enormous broadening of the capacity to experience. When men accept their need to be loved because they *feel* it, they can also learn how to relate to the feelings of others. The transitional nontraditional phase is a rocky road. But one worth taking. Men who make the journey from traditional self-orientation and insensitivity to interdependence and emotions are able to enjoy the Me in their world while genuinely loving others.

While nontraditional women are always self-oriented, they also fall into two groups. The most important characteristic of one group is their ambition. These women have decided that, for now, they don't want the responsibilities of emotionally important relationships. They're unwilling to compromise their freedom to be ambitious.

The most important characteristic of the other group is their rage. Unlike psychologically traditional women, angry nontraditional women say, "The only person you can trust is yourself." The anger often results from divorce and the feeling their trust and love have been betrayed. "I was married for 18 years and my husband left me for someone else. No one is ever going to be able to hurt me like that again." Sometimes the anger comes from their judgment that their life has been empty even though they were always very "good." Often there's a period in which they blame society, their husbands, and their children for entrapping them. But, especially today, it's very common for them to develop goals and a sense of Me. The angry phase is thus an intermediate period of movement toward the interdependent stance.

A permanent self-orientation in women is rare, their socialization continuously pressures them to be feminine, loving, and loved. For most women, being self-oriented (whether angry or career-driven) is temporary; it ends when they recover from divorce or achieve some substantial career success.

Psychologically traditional women whose lives have become unsatisfactory *have to get past their depression and work through their anger.* Psychologically traditional men whose lives have become unsatisfactory *have to get past their anger and work through their depression.* Those in the midst of psychological crisis, those desperately trying to leave life's plateau, may thus have a period of several years in which they are *transitionally* nontraditional. This period of change can be very confusing . . . and hell to live with.

This transition period is usually an intermediate point in the development from a traditional psychological core to a complex or interdependent one. Interdependent people have achieved the integration of feminine and masculine ways of being in the world. When women and men accomplish that task and untie the emotional knots from the past, they are much better able to acknowledge reality, leave life's plateau, and create a satisfying future.

Interdependent People

Interdependent people are psychologically complex. It is common to find, from midlife on, that many people change in this way. Men get vastly more invested in their relationships, allowing themselves to become aware of their need to be loved and to love. As men find themselves comfortable and secure in the sense that they are men, and they don't have to prove it to anybody any more, they become willing to experience tender emotions. Women do the same thing, but in reverse. They become increasingly independent, assertive, and goal-directed. Confident in themselves as women, they are able to leave a narrow concept of self and go into a sector of being that they had previously associated with men.

The really revolutionary aspect of feminism was its challenge to women's traditional priorities and way of viewing themselves. It was a statement that being psychologically and economically dependent is a woeful way to live. The original message underlying the theme that women should earn their own living was that men's lives and self-oriented ways of viewing the world should become the new model for women.

But men and women have a tendency to live together, and it's very hard to have two self-oriented people in the same household. That was not the answer. Rather quickly, the idea developed that the ideal woman and man combined characteristics that were traditionally associated with both sexes. Because feminism has affected many more women than men, women are making these changes more swiftly and in larger numbers than are men. In every age group, far more women than men are interdependent and far more men than women are psychologically traditional.

The major values and attitudes of interdependent women and men are essentially the same. Interdependent people have a clear sense of I, of who they are, and they do things in order to enhance their self-esteem and their self-interests. In that sense, at least some of the time and in some activities, they are self-oriented. But interdependent people are also other-oriented. They acknowledge their need to be in relationships. They don't feel diminished by their need for love and therefore they're not defensive about it. The result is they're able to be sensitive to their own feelings as well as those of others. These people know and are comfortable with the fact that they are both independent and dependent.

Interdependent people are aware of their needs and what they want to do, but they are not self-absorbed, endlessly preoccupied with questions of how they feel and where they're going. They commit to relationships and make them a focus of their lives, but they acknowledge their ambivalence about doing that. They say, "Realistically, that cuts into my freedom and adds to my responsibilities. But, on the whole, I'm happier with the commitment than without it." Whereas at times they may require emotional support or a lot of psychological space, on balance they're neither dependent nor dominating. They accept their sometime needs to be independent and self-oriented and their sometime needs to be cared for and other-oriented.

Interdependent people are often very ambitious in terms of their careers, but they will compromise their self-oriented goals if those objectives jeopardize the well-being of people who are emotionally important to them. An interdependent person would say, "My career is very important to me and I must say your offer is very tempting. But before I can accept it, I have to discuss the ramifications of it with my husband/wife. It's a marvelous opportunity but I can see that it will require a lot of traveling and an enormous amount of work. That would have a tremendous impact on my family, so that's a decision we have to make together." The interdependent couple is made up of peers who respect as well as love each other and, therefore, their decision-making powers are equal. This is very different from psychologically traditional couples in which women are often loved but less frequently respected.

Interdependent people tend to have multiple commitments, and no single commitment outweighs any other over the long term. Their lives are balanced; they give time and psychological energy to their spouse or lover, their children, and their work. Ideally, they are similarly involved with friends, their physical well-being, and their own maturation.

It's not uncommon for men to become interdependent when they're middle-aged and no longer totally absorbed in their careers. When they're less preoccupied with the outside world, they become more aware of their internal emotional experiences. At work, they can become very involved as mentors of younger people; at home, they are vastly more emotionally giving with their grandchildren than they were with their children.

It's even more common to see women, from their late thirties on, become interdependent. They become more assertive and initiating, and many develop serious career interests. At that point "going to work" is different than it was in the earlier years, when they worked to earn a down payment on a house. In the wake of feminism, women are entering the labor force with self-motives and self-perceptions. Plateaued in life in their middle years, they undertake a second career and gain a new sense of themselves.

New Success

When we're young, we imagine that when we're grown, we will really know what we want. It's disconcerting to realize that we never stop learning and growing and changing; nothing is ever settled forever. Many of us are living very differently now from what we once expected. Some of us feel good: we are more complex than we ever thought we'd be, and our lives are rich. Others feel frightened: we have lost the comfort of knowing what we should do and be like. Some of us are still in transition: plateaued, we are struggling to create a new life phase and a new sense of who we are.

The probability of being and feeling plateaued is highest among people who have only one major commitment. And that's mostly men. Because they have not *had* to cope with as many commitments as women who are married, mothers, and in the labor force, the percentage of men who are psychologically traditional, invested in only one commitment, is higher than the percentage of women in every age group. As harassed and overextended as working wife–mothers may feel, many are relatively protected from being plateaued in life because they are psychologically interdependent. Both sexes, and people of all ages, are in danger of being plateaued; but men, especially those in middle age, are consistently more vulnerable.

Even more than changing what we do, changing our basic self takes courage. Some people don't change; they indraw psychologically and they withdraw from reality. When they do that, when they insist on being in the-world-that-was, they increasingly lose any sense that they can cope with the risks that come from change. But life *does* change; that is inexorable. Those who resist change most, who freeze their minds and ways of living, are wholly unprepared for life. When people insist on staying the same and holding off all the unpredictables that will occur, they can't cope with any. We gain the courage to change by being willing to alter how we see ourselves, by changing what we want, and by changing how we live.

Our continuous growth into more complex people is the basis for the courage we need in order to live most fully. Most of us change when we plateau in our old commitments and find they are no longer satisfying. We change because there's not enough good in our present lives and so we set out on voyages of exploration and self-discovery.

That's appropriate and desirable. It's also usually scary, and occasionally delicious. And, we have to remember that while it's tough on us, it's often even harder on those we are close to because *our* changes require that *they* change—and it's not even their voyage! We have to remain aware that we are asking a very great deal from those who are affected by our changing what we do, what we want, and what we are.

Mostly, we need to have the knowledge and conviction that we *can* change and we *do* have choices. Most of us started our adult lives psychologically traditional, and that is why we made the choices we did. When we are psychologically more complex, when we are interdependent, we have many more options to choose from. The breadth of what we will be willing to do, and the experiences we are capable of having, expand greatly when we are better able to move from traditional gender rules of what we can and cannot do.

When people are more complex, they are far better able to redefine success so that it need never end. Most people constrict their experiences and distort their lives in order to achieve traditional success. For many people, that does not seem too great a cost until further success eludes them. At that point, they assay their lives. Then they may either remain in mourning for what they cannot have or they may turn toward the wealth of experiences they never knew. As they give up old values, they are able to develop new ones that can create profound satisfaction. Most fundamentally, as interdependent people, they will reconceptualize a successful person as *someone who continues to engage in life and live fully.*

Every choice we ever made selected one or a few options from among many. Every choice gave us an opportunity and precluded many others. We have all had far fewer experiences than the total range that exists. Every choice we ever made, every role we ever went into, gave us something and excluded much more. So that which we have never done, that which we have never become, is really ours to gain, especially from midlife on.

The broader the range of our experiences, the wider our capacities to experience. When we are complex, interdependent people, engaged in a range of experiences, committed in some aspects of our lives and experimental in others, we are in the best of positions. We can initiate change, so there is always some challenge. We need never be plateaued in life.

Appendix A

Questions to Ask Yourself

These are "study questions," designed to help you assess how you feel about work and life in general. Answering them should give you a clearer idea of how you feel and whether you need to create changes.

Plateauing at Work

1. How long have you held your present position? How long did you, or do you, expect to remain in it?
2. Was your last job change a promotion, a lateral change, or a demotion? If it wasn't a promotion, how did that make you feel?
3. Do you expect further promotions? When? Do you know what position(s) you would be eligible for?
4. Were you ever fast-track? Are you now? If you were, and are not now, how do you feel about that?
5. Are you basically competent and dependable—neither a star nor in a slump? Is that okay with you?
6. What is the best thing that's happened to you at work in the last year? Why do you think it's the best? Can you get more of that kind of success?
7. What's the worst thing that's happened in the past year? Why do you consider it so terrible? Are you likely to have that experience again?

8. Is your organization a good place for you? Answer the following questions and make a judgment about the fit between your personality and the climate of the organization.

   Is decision-making participative or top-down?
   Is it what you know or who you know that matters?
   Are new ideas and initiatives welcome?
   Is the mood personal or pretty distant between people?
   Are the most successful people risk-creators?
   Is it presumed that work takes precedence over everything else?

9. Overall, do you think you belong in your organization?
10. In what specific ways are you satisfied with the work you are doing?
11. In what specific ways is the work unsatisfying?
12. Which feels greater, the amount of satisfaction or dissatisfaction?
13. Can you change what you do so you can get more satisfaction?
14. Have you tried to do that? If not, why not?
15. What are the three most important things you need from your work? Rate the extent to which those needs are satisfied.
16. Do you need challenge? Do you get it at work? Do you need more?
17. What can you do to get more challenge at work? Be specific in your answer. Think, for example, about a lateral transfer, a demotion, formal education, a restructuring of your position with others.
18. How long do you think you will be satisfied doing the work you're doing? If you think you need a change, what will you do to make that happen? What will you do if it does not happen?
19. To what extent does your work give your life meaning and purpose? Does it satisfy your ideals? Is it the only thing in life that does?
20. Are you a workaholic? If you are, does that disturb you? Does it bother you enough to change how you live?
21. Are you willing to work harder than you are, about the same, or less?
22. What kind of "success" do you need? At this time in your life, do you need more traditional success or is a balanced life more important?
23. Would more success, of the kinds you've already had, take you in the direction of personal growth you want?

24. If the answer to question 23 is no, what kinds of work changes would do that?
25. At work, are you a risk-avoider, risk-taker, or risk-creator? Does risk frighten you or get you charged up?
26. Do you prefer to initiate changes or run an ongoing project?
27. Does failure make you depressed—or angry and energized?
28. When you think about how you relate to risk, what does that teach you about the work you're comfortable with? What are the implications in terms of how much responsibility and power you're likely to be given?
29. Have you ever had a big change in the kind of work you do? How did you react to that?
30. How important is a promotion to you?
31. What do you want that only a promotion can give you?
33. Are you structurally plateaued?
34. Are you content plateaued?
35. Would a lateral transfer with new responsibilities and an increase in money satisfy you?
36. Could you accept a demotion if your work changed and your salary remained stable?
37. Have you remained current in your work through education?
38. Have you seriously considered a second career? Are you prepared to leave your organization?
39. Are you ready for retirement? Do you need to work?
40. What are your special assets at work? Which ones are transferable to other kinds of work or other organizations?

Plateauing in Life

1. Does your life feel repetitive?
2. Is your life too predictable?
3. Do you need some sector in which you begin something new, in which you can't know exactly what will happen?
4. Do you feel weighed down by responsibilities?
5. Do you feel trapped by the habits of how you live?
6. If you feel weighed down or trapped, is that the result of factors you cannot change or the result of your own fear or guilt?
5. Do you have any commitments that create a future for you?
6. What are you good at?
7. What are you interested in?
8. What do you most like to do?

9. What do you do for fun?
10. Can you create a new commitment or increase an old one that has these positive qualities?
11. Is your spouse your friend?
12. Do you have friends?
13. Are you emotionally close to your children?
14. Do you talk about what's important to you? Whom do you talk to?
15. Do you contaminate your personal life with work? Do you need to learn how to relax?
16. Are you comfortable only with people who do work like yours?
17. What nonwork activities do or could give you pleasure and expand your experiences?
18. In what spheres of your life is your goal contentment? Excitement? Do you achieve either?
19. Do you need to change the percentage of time you give to your commitments? What do your spouse or your children or your friends say?
20. Is aging an issue you have to deal with?
21. Do you respect the person you have become? If not, what would it take?
22. Do you need to become less self-absorbed or more self-directed?
23. Do you take time for yourself?
24. Are you comfortable with your body? Do you exercise?
25. Do you have goals for your core self? Are you moving toward them or are you blocked?
26. If you are blocked, can you figure a way to move past that? If not, are you willing to seek professional help?
27. Do you feel that you have a lot of control over what happens to you?
28. Are you essentially active or passive in terms of making things happen?
29. Are you lonely or rich in relationships?
30. Do you allow yourself to become aware of how you feel?
31. Basically, are you living the kind of life you want to live?
32. Do you have regrets about what you have done?
33. Do you have regrets about what you have not done?
34. Do you accept your limitations and respect your assets?
35. Considering the realities of life and the compromises that are inevitable, can you say you are fulfilled?

Appendix B

Checklist of Plateauing Symptoms

Passiveness	Signal			Change	
	Weak	Moderate	Strong	Yes	No
An "I don't care" attitude about work. Noninvolvement.					
Withdrawal from people socially or in terms of working with them.					
A lack of initiative.					
A lack of energy.					
Having no specific goals and no time frame.					
Passive forms of aggression, involving overt agreement but basic noncompliance.					
Inability to make decisions.					

Work Symptom	Signal			Change	
	Weak	Moderate	Strong	Yes	No
An increase in the number of hours worked, with no increase in output.					
Due dates being missed.					
Work needing to be redone.					
Incomplete work.					
Routine tasks taking much longer.					
Work being put off.					
Doing only what is required.					
No new ideas.					
An increase in the number of errors.					
Insisting on doing things the old way.					
Coming late and leaving early.					
Never being in a hurry.					
No follow through.					
Being hung up in details.					
Prolonging decisions.					
Being obsessed with rules.					
Things just not getting done.					

General	Signal			Change	
	Weak	Moderate	Strong	Yes	No
An increase in illness.					
Inappropriate dress.					
Being critical of others.					
A tendency to withdraw from others.					
Insisting on being the leader.					
Refusing the leadership role.					
Not volunteering.					
Not helping others.					
Insisting things be done your way.					
Refusing to give an opinion.					
No energy or chronic fatigue.					
A lack of initiative.					
Marked weight gain or loss for no obvious reason.					
Using drugs or a heavy use of alcohol or tobacco.					
A tendency to fly off the handle.					
Tension or irritability.					
A loss of sense of humor.					
Excessive amounts of putdown humor.					

	Signal			Change	
	Weak	Moderate	Strong	Yes	No
Minor problems being very upsetting.					
Fears you never had before.					
Mistrust of others.					
A feeling of urgency about time.					
Seeking reassurance you are liked.					
Forgetfulness.					
Living in the past, in the good old days.					
No sense of what's really important.					
Pushiness or hostility.					
The feeling of being excluded.					
No long-range perspective.					

Busyness

Working very long hours, but not productively or creatively.					
A quality of busyness at work.					
Complaining of being too busy at home.					
Complaining of being too busy to have time for self.					

Notes

This is a combination footnotes and bibliography section. References are numbered in alphabetical order. Footnote numbers in the text refer to these references.

1. Alsop, Ronald, "Mixed Bag: As Early Retirement Grows in Popularity, Some Have Misgivings," *Wall Street Journal* (April 24, 1984), pp. 1, 20.
2. "Baby Boomers Push for Power," *Business Week* (July 2, 1984), pp. 52-62.
3. Bardwick, Judith M., "The Dynamics of Successful People," *New Research on Women*, ed. D. McGuigan (Ann Arbor: University of Michigan Press, 1974), pp. 86-104
4. Bardwick, Judith M., *In Transition* (New York: Holt, Rinehart and Winston, 1979).
5. Bardwick, Judith M., "Middle Age and a Sense of Future," *Merrill-Palmer Quarterly*, Vol. 24, No. 2 (April 1978), pp. 3-8.
6. Bardwick, Judith M., "Plateauing and Productivity," *Sloan Management Review* (Spring 1983), pp. 67-73.
7. Bardwick, Judith M., "Seasons of a Woman's Life," *Women's Lives*, ed. D. McGuigan (Ann Arbor: University of Michigan Press, 1980), pp. 35-58.
8. Bartolome', Fernando, "Executives as Human Beings," *Harvard Business Review* (November-December 1972), reprinted in *Executives in Mid-Career*, pp. 21-28.
9. Bartolome', Fernando, "The Work Alibi: When It's Harder to Go Home," *Harvard Business Review* (March-April 1983), pp. 67-74.
10. Benson, Herbert, and Robert L. Allen, "How Much Stress Is Too Much?" *Harvard Business Review* (September-October 1980), pp. 86-92.
11. Boone, Timothy, "Mike—Senior Partner," unpublished interview, 1984.
12. Carlson, Elliot, "The Plateau-Makers," *Dynamic Years* (March-April 1985), pp. 28-35.
13. Connor, Samuel R., and John S. Fielden, "Rx for Managerial Shelf

Sitters," *Harvard Business Review* (November-December 1973), pp. 113-120.

14. Dalton, Gene W., and Paul H. Thompson, "Accelerating Obsolescence of Older Engineers," *Harvard Business Review* (September-October 1971), reprinted in *Executives in Mid-Career*, pp. 127-137.

15. Davis, Stanley M., and Roger L. Gould, "Three Vice Presidents in Mid-Life," *Harvard Business Review* (July-August 1981), pp. 118-130.

16. Denison, Daniel R., "Bringing Corporate Culture to the Bottom Line," *Organizational Dynamics* (Autumn 1984), pp. 5-22.

17. Drucker, Peter F., "Executives are 'Aging' at 42," *Wall Street Journal* (March 7, 1984), pp. 1-2.

18. Fenn, Dan H., Jr., "Executives as Community Volunteers," *Harvard Business Review* (March-April 1971), reprinted in *Executives in Mid-Career*, pp. 139-148.

19. Ferguson, Lawrence L., "Better Management of Managers' Careers," *Harvard Business Review* (March-April 1966), reprinted in *Executives in Mid-Career*, pp. 67-80.

20. Fowler, Elizabeth M., "Careers—Graduates Face Job Scarcity," *New York Times* (June 8, 1983), p. D17.

21. Gerstein, Marc, and Heather Resiman, "Strategic Selection: Matching Executives to Business Conditions," *Sloan Management Review* (Winter 1983), pp. 33-49.

22. "GM to Cut Redundant Jobs," *San Diego Union* (August 12, 1984), p. A-4.

23. Goldman, Robert, "Getting Stuck on the Way Up the Corporate Ladder," *Wall Street Journal* (January 6, 1986), p. 20.

24. Gottschalk, Earl C., Jr., "Blocked Paths: Promotions Grow Few as Baby Boom Group Eyes Managers' Jobs," *Wall Street Journal* (October 22, 1981), p. 1.

25. Granelli, James S., "Lawyers' Numbers Boom as Age Drops," *Los Angeles Times* (February 18, 1984), pp. 1, 8.

26. Green, Cynthia, "Middle Managers Are Still Sitting Ducks," *Business Week* (September 16, 1985), p. 34.

27. Hardis, Stephen R., personal conversation with author (October 1984).

28. James, Barrie G., "SMR Forum: Strategic Planning Under Fire," *Sloan Management Review*, (Summer 1984), pp. 57-61.

29. Jenkins, Roger L., Richard C. Reizenstein, and F. G. Rodgers, "Report Cards on the MBA," *Harvard Business Review* (September-October 1984), pp. 20-30.

30. Johnston, Oswald, "Boomers Redefining Job Success," *Los Angeles Times* (October 19, 1985), pp. 1, 8.

31. Katz, Ralph, "Time and Work: Toward An Integrative Perspective," *Research in Organizational Behavior*, Vol. 2 (1980), pp. 81-127.

32. Kofodimos, Joan R., "A Question of Balance," *Issues & Observations*, Vol. 4, No. 1 (February 1984), pp. 1-9.

33. Kotter, John P., "What Effective General Managers Really Do," *Harvard Business Review* (November-December 1982), pp. 156-167.
34. Lauenstein, Milton C., "Cutting Companies Down to Size," *Harvard Business Review* (September-October 1984), pp. 6-14.
35. Lehner, Urban C., and John Marcom, Jr., "Auto Automation," *Wall Street Journal* (July 9, 1984), pp. 1, 14.
36. Lekachman, Robert, "Times Board of Economists: A Critical Look at Reagan's Record," *Los Angeles Times* (October 30, 1984), p. IV-3.
37. Levinson, Daniel J., *Seasons of a Man's Life* (New York: Alfred A. Knopf, 1978).
38. Levinson, Harry, "When Executives Burn Out," *Harvard Business Review* (May-June 1981), pp. 74-81.
39. Longman, Phillip, "The Downwardly Mobile Baby Boomers," *Wall Street Journal* (April 12, 1985), p. 33.
40. "Long Term Outlook for the U.S. Economy," Security Pacific Bank/ Monthly Summary of Business Conditions, *Southern California*, Economics Department, Vol. 63, No. 8 (August 1984).
41. Louv, Richard, "New Baby Boomers—A 'Designer Kid Syndrome,'" *The San Diego Union* (December 29, 1985), p. A-3.
42. "MBA Graduates May Face Lean Times," *San Diego Union* (October 8, 1984), p. A-19.
43. McLean, Alan A., *Work Stress* (Reading, Mass.: Addison-Wesley Publishing Co., 1979).
44. "Mid-Life Crisis," *Yale Alumni Magazine and Journal*, Vol. XLIII, No. 8 (June 1980), pp. 30-31.
45. Miller, William H., "Who'll Replace the Vanishing Vets?" *Industry Week* (April 16, 1984), pp. 46-50.
46. Naisbitt, John, *Megatrends* (New York: Warner Books, 1984).
47. Nemiroff, R. A., and C. A. Colarusso, *The Race Against Time* (New York: Plenum Press, 1985).
48. Niehouse, Oliver L., "Measuring Your Burnout Potential," *Supervisory Management* (July 1984), pp. 27-33.
49. Niehouse, Oliver L., and Matt Mihovich, "Setting Up an In-House Program for the Rehabilitation of Burnout Victims," *Management Review* (February 1984), pp. 27-43.
50. Patton, A., "The Coming Flood of Young Executives," *Harvard Business Review* (September-October 1976), pp. 1-6.
51. Peter, Laurence J., and Raymond Hull, *The Peter Principle* (New York: William Morrow and Co., Inc., 1969).
52. "Portrait of America, A," *Newsweek* (January 17, 1983), pp. 20-33.
53. Powell, William J., Jr., and Steven E. Prokesch, "White-Collar Jobs: A Hot Market Cools," *Business Week* (December 10, 1984), pp. 40, 41.
54. Quinn, Robert E., and Patricia L. Lees, "Attraction and Harassment: Dynamics of Sexual Politics in the Workplace," *Organizational Dynamics* (Autumn 1984), pp. 35-46.
55. *Research Institute Recommendations* (September 28, 1984), pp. 3-4.

56. Robinette, Hillary M., "The Police Problem Employee," *FBI Law Enforcement Bulletin* (July 1982), pp. 1-8.

57. Rogan, Helen, "Executive Women Find It Difficult to Balance Demands of Job, Home," *Wall Street Journal* (October 30, 1984), p. 33.

58. Rosen, Benson, and Thomas H. Jerdee, "Too Old or Not Too Old," *Harvard Business Review* (November-December 1977), pp. 97-106.

59. Schreiner, Tim, "A Revolution That Has Just Begun," *USA Today* (May 29, 1984), p. 4D.

60. Schumer, Fran R., "Downward Mobility," *New York Magazine* (August 16, 1982), pp. 19-26.

61. Shearer, L., "Critical Age for Women," *Parade Magazine* (August 5, 1984), p. 15.

62. Stoner, James A. F., et al., *Managerial Career Plateaus* (New York: Center for Research in Career Development, Graduate School of Business, Columbia University, 1980).

63. "Teaching New Tricks," *Training* (December 1984), p. 114.

64. Towill, "Productivity Drift in Extended Learning Curves," *OMEGA*, Vol. 6, No. 4 (1978), pp. 295-304.

65. U.S. Department of Labor's Bureau of Labor Statistics, "Tomorrow's Jobs," *Occupational Outlook Handbook*, 1982-1983 ed. (April 1982).

66. Veiga, John, "Do Managers on the Move Get Anywhere?" *Harvard Business Review* (March-April 1981), pp. 20-38.

67. Warren, E. Kirby, Thomas P. Ference, and James A. F. Stoner, "Case of the Plateaued Performer," Harvard Business Review (January-February 1975) pp. 30-38, 146-147.

68. "Women Now One-Third of All First-Year Medical Students," *San Diego Union* (September 28, 1984), p. A-16.

69. Yao, Margaret, "Middle-Aged Officials Find New Group Hit by Slump: Themselves," *Wall Street Journal* (September 1, 1982), pp. 1, 14.

70. Zemke, Ron, "The Case of the Missing Managerial Malaise," *Training* (November 1985), pp. 30-33.

71. Zemke, Ron, "To Train Baby Boom Managers, Learn What Makes Them Tick," *Training/HRD* (December 1980), pp. 36-40.

Index